A GAME FOR HIGH STAKES

A GAME FOR HIGH STAKES

Lessons Learned in Negotiating with the Soviet Union

Edited by
Leon Sloss *and*
M. Scott Davis

Ballinger Publishing Company
Cambridge, Massachusetts
A Subsidiary of Harper & Row, Publishers, Inc.

International Standard Book Number: 0-88730-072-3

Library of Congress Catalog Card Number: 85-18630

Printed in the United States of America

Library of Congress Cataloging-in-Publication Data

Main entry under title:

A Game for high stakes.

   Bibliography: p.
   Includes index.
   1. United States—Foreign relations—Soviet Union.
2. Soviet Union—Foreign relations—United States.
3. Negotiation. I. Sloss, Leon. II. Davis, M. Scott.
JX1428.S65G35   1985   327.47'073   85-18630
ISBN 0-88730-072-3

Roosevelt Center for American Policy Studies

The Roosevelt Center is a nonprofit, nonpartisan, public policy institute with offices in Washington, D.C. and Chicago, Illinois. Its goals are to clarify the policy choices before the nation and to encourage and facilitate the participation of citizens in the decision-making process at all levels of government. The Center's program develops a comprehensive range of reasoned options and strategies concerning critical policy issues facing the United States.

In all cases, the Center maintains a strictly nonpartisan posture. This decision to forgo the more traditional institutional approach of advocating particular policy alternatives was carefully made. It stems from a bedrock belief that the genius of American society springs from a free market in ideas, and that policy decisionmaking should be no exception.

Founded in 1982, the Roosevelt Center takes its name and inspiration from three Roosevelts — Theodore, Eleanor, and Franklin — who courageously addressed our nation's future and brought clarity to America's vision of itself.

CONTENTS

LIST OF ABBREVIATIONS

ABM	antiballistic missile
ACDA	Arms Control and Disarmament Agency
ASAT	antisatellite
BATNA	best alternative to a negotiated agreement
CD	Conference on Disarmament
CDE	Conference on Disarmament in Europe
CSCE	Conference on Security and Cooperation in Europe
CTB	comprehensive test ban
DOD	Department of Defense
DOE	Department of Energy
EEC	European Economic Community
ENDC	Eighteen National Disarmament Conference
GAC	President's General Advisory Committee on Arms Control and Disarmament
GKNT	State Committee on Science and Technology (Soviet Union)
INF	intermediate-range nuclear forces
JCS	Joint Chiefs of Staff
MBFR	Mutual and Balanced Force Reductions
MIRV	multiple independently-targetable reentry vehicle
MLF	Multilateral Force
NATO	North Atlantic Treaty Organization

NCA	National Command Authority
NPT	Nuclear Non-Proliferation Treaty
NSC	National Security Council
OSD	Office of the Secretary of Defense
PAC	political action committee
PNE	peaceful nuclear explosion
SALT	Strategic Arms Limitation Talks (or Treaty)
SCC	Standing Consultative Commission
SHAPE	Supreme Headquarters Allied Powers, Europe
SPC	Senior Political Committee
START	Strategic Arms Reduction Talks
TNF	theater nuclear forces

PREFACE

This volume is the outgrowth of a series of seminars entitled "Lessons Learned in Negotiating with the Soviet Union" held under the auspices of the Roosevelt Center for American Policy Studies between May and July 1984. The project has two broad objectives. The first is to identify and reflect upon those lessons learned from our multiple experiences in negotiating with the Soviet Union that could usefully be applied to future negotiations. In reviewing the past, there is no substitute for seeking out the recollections of those with first-hand experience. It is not uncommon for U.S. negotiators to be thrust into situations with little prior preparation for dealing with the Soviets. One experienced negotiator who has dealt with arms control for many years pointed out that we have to relearn constantly lessons that had already been learned. Thus, assembling and recording in an organized form the reflections of seasoned negotiators should provide a resource of great value to their successors.

A second objective of the project is to explain for the general public the nature of the negotiating process between the United States and the Soviet Union, one of the most crucial endeavors of our time. These negotiations differ in important respects from other types of negotiations in that they are between adversary superpowers, both with the capability to destroy the world. They are certainly different from those conducted by two or more parties within our own society or those with allies. They are even different from negotiations with other adversaries, given the dominant role of the two superpowers in world affairs. A better understanding of the peculiarities of U.S.–Soviet negotiations will lead to a better public appreciation of what can and cannot be accomplished through such negotiations. This appreciation is important in helping inform Americans and empowering them to participate in their nation's decisionmaking on the key policy issues in the U.S.–Soviet relationship.

Participants in the seminar series were primarily experienced in planning and conducting arms control negotiations. However, several have been involved in commercial and agricultural negotiations with the Soviets and others have studied the practice and techniques of negotiation and, in some cases, applied those techniques in other settings, such as labor–management negotiations. The participants, who are listed in the Appendix, held a variety of views about the possibilities and problems of negotiating with the Soviet Union. On some points, there was a broad consensus; on others, clear differences emerged. All agreed on the need for more careful examination and analysis—in the Soviet Union as well as the United States—of the problems inherent in this process.

The first chapter of this book is an introduction and a distillation of the main findings from the presentations and discussions, pointing out major areas of agreement and disagreement. The following chapters are either papers presented at the seminars or edited texts of oral presentations. Substantive footnotes reflect discussion of key points at the seminars and were added by the editors rather than the individual authors.

The conclusions chapter reflects the views of the seminars' Chairman, Leon Sloss, and not necessarily those of any of the other participants. As the designer and principal implementer of the series, he was in a unique position to draw special lessons from the overall enterprise. His conclusions are presented in that spirit.

I am particularly grateful to the book's fourteen contributors for their willingness to share with other negotiators and the public their reflections on this critical component of American political history. Mastering the craft of superpower negotiations is a challenge to America—and to the Soviet Union. The problems they must solve together—or lead in solving—in order to create a more stable and secure world are enormous. The contributors to this book (and their

Soviet counterparts) have played a critical role in seeking solutions to these problems. But there is much work yet to be done.

In addition to the contributors to the book, a number of people deserve special thanks for their efforts on this project. Invaluable guidance, both conceptual and managerial, was provided by Michael Higgins and Christopher Makins of the Roosevelt Center. Scott Davis was the book's overall editor, and Wendy Russell served as its marketing agent. Dean Millot's comments on the first and last chapters were very helpful. Rick Buchanan, Patrick Higgins, and David Sloss provided able assistance with editing and research. Monica Andres contributed her always-efficient library services, and Kathy Black and Sue Leander endured the seemingly endless typing of drafts of the chapters.

Let us hope that the efforts of these individuals can help lead to greater U.S. skill in negotiating with the Soviet Union—and a more constructive U.S.–Soviet relationship.

Roger Molander, President
Roosevelt Center for American
    Policy Studies
Washington, D.C.
June 1985

1 LESSONS LEARNED IN NEGOTIATING WITH THE SOVIET UNION
Introduction and Findings

Leon Sloss

On March 12, 1985, the United States and the Soviet Union resumed negotiations on nuclear forces after a hiatus in talks of over a year. The deployment of U.S. missiles in Europe had been the proximate cause of the breakdown in 1983 in the negotiations on intermediate- and long-range nuclear forces, INF and START, respectively. However, substantial policy differences over a wide variety of politico-military issues have long kept the United States and the Soviet Union from reaching major accords on arms. On the other hand, each super-power is interested in continuing a dialogue on ways to reduce the risk of war. Even during the tense period surrounding the cancellation of nuclear arms talks in late 1983, negotiations involving the two superpowers and others on conventional and other arms issues continued in Vienna, Geneva, and Stockholm.

The 1985 negotiations in Geneva cover not only intermediate- and long-range nuclear weapons, but also space weapons. Already the talks have bogged down on the question of whether agreements in any single area should be concluded without a package deal covering all three. Indeed, fundamental disagreements about these weapons suggest that the negotiations will be protracted, perhaps lasting years, as was the case with the Strategic Arms Limitation Treaty (SALT) talks in the 1970s.

In conducting these and other negotiations, including not only those on arms but also on commerce and other exchanges, we should

1

be prepared to draw upon the past experience of U.S.-Soviet negotiations. The history of such discussions is extensive, not only on arms control but on other diplomatic and commercial negotiations as well. However, the written record is fragmentary and often anecdotal (see Bibliography). A vast accumulated experience, residing in the memories of individuals, remains largely untapped. There is much to be learned from examining this experience systematically. This volume, the product of a series of seminars called "Lessons Learned in Negotiating with the Soviet Union," held in Washington, D.C., during the summer of 1984, provides such an examination.

Improving the techniques and skills of U.S. negotiators may increase the prospect of achieving agreements that will enhance U.S. security. While negotiating skills constitute only a fraction of the key factors involved in a negotiation, they are essential. And, unlike many other factors bearing on the outcome of a negotiation, our negotiating skills can be improved unilaterally. In particular, a better understanding of Soviet negotiating objectives, style, technique, processes, and personnel could support a more effective U.S. approach to arms control talks. Such knowledge can also help the public to appreciate the conditions U.S. negotiators confront in the arms control negotiations process.

GENERAL OBSERVATIONS

Neither experts nor the American public agrees on the role, importance, and priority of arms control in U.S. security policy. This disagreement affects views about how arms control should be negotiated, especially about the urgency of reaching agreement. To illustrate, two "typical views" can be contrasted. The first expresses concern that arms control does not play a sufficiently important role in security policy, say, in decisions about weapons systems and how to deal with the Soviet Union. In this view, if the United States were only more aggressive in advancing proposals and in seeking compromises, greater progress could be made toward reaching agreements. For example, the Independent Commission on Disarmament and Security Issues, a prestigious international group chaired by Swedish Prime Minister Olaf Palme and including former U.S. Secretary of State Cyrus Vance, said the following in 1982:

We believe there is an urgent need for agreements specifying major reductions of nuclear weapons and restraints on their qualitative improvements.... The process of strategic arms limitation is indispensable. It is important too because it has become a key factor in the relations between the United States and the Soviet Union, affecting the very framework and climate of international relations.... Negotiations must be resumed without preconditions and further delay.[1]

The second view, by contrast, is concerned that the effort to reach negotiated arms control settlements with the Soviet Union has been overly dominant in shaping decisions on strategy and weapons programs. This view maintains that the Soviets use arms control cynically—principally to manipulate opinion in the West by creating public pressures on Western governments to curb necessary arms programs. For example, a recent study sponsored by the Department of Defense on ballistic missile defense, entitled "The Future Security Strategy Study," states: "Current Soviet policy on arms agreements is dominated by the Soviet Union's attempts to derive unilateral advantage from arms negotiations and agreements, by accepting only arrangements that permit continued Soviet increases in military strength while using the negotiation process to inhibit Western increases in military strength."[2]

These differences over the role and importance of arms control, in turn, lead to differences over the proper tactics for dealing with the Soviet Union in negotiations. Some commentators hold that because we have appeared too eager in the past to reach agreements, we have reached unsatisfactory agreements. Instead, *the United States should take "tough" positions in negotiations and stick with them,* forcing the other side to compromise, even if that necessitated prolonged negotiations. Director of the U.S. Arms Control and Disarmament Agency Kenneth Adelman reflected this view when he said after the Soviet walkout of November 1983, "I don't think we should give any concessions to the Soviets to bring them back to the talks.... I think that's just a bad way to proceed in any kind of negotiation."[3]

Others are fearful that by appearing intransigent we will undermine any prospect for a successful negotiation. They believe that

1. *The New York Times,* June 2, 1982, p. 10.
2. U.S., Department of Defense, *Ballistic Missile Defense and U.S. National Security,* Fred S. Hoffman, Study Director (Washington, D.C.: Government Printing Office, October 1983), p. 11.
3. *Wall Street Journal,* April 30, 1984, p. 35.

forthcoming positions will improve the climate and, thus, the prospect for successful negotiation. In this view, reaching agreement is an important objective. On returning from a visit to Moscow in the spring of 1984, Senators William Cohen (R.-Maine) and Joseph Biden (D.-Delaware) urged the Reagan administration to take some arms control initiatives outside the field of nuclear arms as a demonstration to the Soviets that the president was serious about resuming bilateral negotiations. Such initiatives, they argued, "would build a better climate for returning to nuclear talks."[4]

A further point of disagreement concerns the extent and significance of asymmetries in U.S. and Soviet objectives and negotiating styles. Some observers stress the asymmetries, while others emphasize common interests and practices. For example, there are those who believe that because Western negotiators are often pressed by public opinion to arrive at agreements, they are placed at a disadvantage in negotiating with the closed and more monolithic states of the communist world in which public opinion plays little role. Others believe that this view exaggerates the significance of asymmetries, and that the Soviets have an equal interest in agreements that could reduce the risk of nuclear war. In this view, neither the United States nor the Soviet Union has a good alternative to negotiations.

These very broad outlooks on arms control affect views about how specific arms control negotiations should be conducted, the value of any agreements reached, and, indeed, the extent to which the United States should seek to resolve its differences with the Soviet Union through the negotiation process. These outlooks inevitably colored opinions expressed during the seminar series, as they color the continuing debate in the United States about the best direction for U.S. policy on arms control. Three of the most frequently discussed questions in the seminars were these:

Should arms control be linked to other issues? A general linkage of arms control to the international climate and U.S.–Soviet relations is inevitable. For example, there was no way that Soviet actions vis-à-vis Afghanistan and, later, Poland could be isolated from the SALT II agreement. However, some participants maintained that specific linkages, such as between arms control and trade agreements, should be avoided wherever possible. They argued that our leverage through trade is limited and arms control is too important to be made hostage

4. *Washington Post,* March 7, 1984, p. A7.

to other conditions. Others believed that arms control should be seen as part of a broader, continuing process of negotiation with the Soviets, that the Soviets view it in this way, and that linkage cannot and should not be avoided. Two participants with experience in commercial negotiations reached different conclusions about linkage. Robert McLellan, vice president for government relations at FMC Corporation, argued that we should use the Soviet desire for commercial relations to secure political, and particularly arms control, benefits; Robert Schmidt, chairman of the board and chief executive officer of Jacob Wind Electric, and the veteran of many commercial negotiations with the Soviets, was more skeptical about the feasibility of such linkage.

How should the United States design its overall strategy for negotiating specific agreements? There was general agreement that the question of how to open negotiations does present a dilemma, indeed two dilemmas. One concerns dealing with the Soviet Union; the other, allied and U.S. domestic politics. If our opening position is close to what we want as an outcome, the Soviets will start negotiating from there and we are likely to end up being pressed to accept an unsatisfactory outcome. If, however, our position is padded with a great deal of room for negotiation, the Soviets may not negotiate seriously but, instead, use the asserted one-sidedness of our proposals as propaganda in the arena of international public opinion. They have done this both in START and INF. With regard to domestic and allied politics, if we open with a "hard" offer and later retreat from that position, we may appear "weak." This could harm prospects for ratification of the agreement. But to open with a "soft" offer and hold firm is to run the risk of being seen as "uncompromising." Most frequently, the United States has opened negotiations with plenty of latitude for bargaining. However, there have been cases, as in SALT II, where our initial offer was close to our final position.

It was suggested that, to avoid this dilemma, we should begin negotiations with exploratory discussions. However, at some point a proposal must be made if there are to be negotiations. The Soviets have traditionally been reluctant to make the first proposal, and thus the United States often had to take the initiative. Another possible approach would be to present certain U.S. principles or interests at the outset of a negotiation and then formulate specific proposals only after the Soviet position has been heard and after intensive exploratory discussion. Clearly, the choice of an opening position should bear close relationship to the strategy and tactics planned for subsequent negotiating rounds. This requires planning ahead—having a "negotiating concept" that avoids the extremes of amicability and hostility.

What is the value of bargaining chips and how should they be used? Most experienced negotiators agree that weapons conceived by the United States solely for the purpose of negotiations do not provide much leverage, while ones we are obviously not prepared to relinquish cannot provide the Soviets with much incentive to discuss arms control. The Soviets show a more serious interest in reaching agreement when there is some U.S. development they wish to halt such as the Safeguard antiballistic missile (ABM) system in 1972 and space-based weapons in 1984. Thus, while the Soviets must have incentives to negotiate, these may be better provided by the overall trend of defense programs and a perceived U.S. commitment to sustain those programs that appear to alter the balance than by weapons systems advertised specifically as bargaining chips.

FINDINGS

Our discussions covered diverse aspects of negotiating including the Soviet approach to negotiations, lessons for future negotiators, multilateral negotiations, the executive–congressional relationship in these matters, and the role of the U.S. bureaucracy. A brief discussion of the findings follows.

Soviet Negotiating Style and Tactics

The Soviet concept of negotiations is broader and differs from that in the West. Former counselor of the State Department and senior member of the National Security Council (NSC) staff Helmut Sonnenfeldt suggested that the Soviets see negotiations as part of a broad effort to secure national interests and use all available means, however remote from the subject of negotiations, to attain their bargaining objectives. The Soviets do not always place a high priority on concluding agreements; sometimes they use the negotiating process to promote broader interests. For example, Soviet leaders manipulate arms talks to influence public opinion in the West and to divide the United States from its allies, as they attempted during the INF negotiations.

Of course, the U.S. government has also used arms control negotiations to advance objectives more general than those of the specific talks at issue. For example, a major American objective of the talks on Mutual and Balanced Force Reductions (MBFR) was to forestall unilateral U.S. troop reductions in Europe. The U.S. decision to pursue INF negotiations was prompted by the need to secure West European support for INF deployments. However, unlike the Soviets, Americans often seem uncomfortable if a negotiation does not conclude with a signed document. American (and European) public opinion tends to measure the results of arms control discussions in terms of whether or not agreements are concluded. Similar public pressures for agreements do not exist in the East.

The Soviets are very sensitive to being treated as equals of the United States. Sonnenfeldt noted that their decision to enter into diplomatic relations with the West in the 1930s was not made lightly. Soviet leaders sought to ensure that when they did join the international diplomatic scene, they and their state would be taken seriously. The Soviets value their military prowess because it ensures their treatment as equals of the United States. To the Soviets, arms control negotiations, and particularly strategic arms negotiations, symbolize their superpower status and place them on a par with the United States, at least militarily. Soviet negotiators clearly expect that position to be recognized and respected. They are very sensitive to any statements or actions that might imply Soviet inferiority. They have shown these same sensitivities in commercial negotiations as well. This concern about form or style might be called the nouveau riche complex, and it precedes the Soviet regime in Russia. While intangible, it is a factor that must be taken into account in negotiations.

While any negotiation is an adversary process, negotiating with the Soviets is unlike negotiating with our allies. There are few common values from which both sides proceed. The experience with negotiation in the two cultures is quite different. Americans draw heavily from the example of labor-management negotiations, in which a shared interest in the ultimate prosperity of the industry or firm gives both sides an incentive to compromise. The Soviet experience is heavily influenced by the peasant–merchant relationship, in which each side can seek maximum advantage with relatively little penalty for either if no deal is concluded. In other words, Americans tend to see negotiations as a relationship in which both sides can end up better off, while the Soviets act as if arms talks are a "zero sum" game in which one side's gain is the other's loss.

Soviet negotiating teams have more continuity than U.S. teams, and this generally gives them an advantage. Soviet negotiators are usually well versed in the details of the negotiations and appear to be willing to wait indefinitely for an agreement that suits them. U.S. negotiators are often impatient to conclude an agreement "on their watch," and the watch is changed frequently. Therefore, it is particularly important for the United States to find ways either to maintain more continuity or to compensate for frequent changes in personnel. Continuity in the backstopping group and in at least some of the negotiating team is highly desirable. But this may not be feasible in the U.S. system, where both political and career assignments tend to last only a few years. Because of this turnover in personnel, careful training and preparation for negotiations is particularly important for the United States.

Soviet arms control positions, like those of the United States, are designed to protect their long-term defense programs. Despite this approach, Soviet programs are not wholly inflexible. For example, the Soviets agreed to limit ABM deployments and dismantled nuclear submarines to stay within the SALT I treaty limits, although, unlike the United States, they have legally converted some of the dismantled submarines to other purposes. However, they are not likely to alter their programs unless they can gain major concessions in return. Thus, the United States will have to be prepared to accept significant limits if it wants significant reductions or limitations on the other side.

Given the reluctance of both sides to limit ongoing programs, arms control agreements that permit gradual change over a period of years and that take into account the different plans of both sides are more likely to be successful. For example, SALT II did provide for phased reductions and did acknowledge the asymmetries in forces by permitting the Soviets to keep their heavy intercontinental ballistic missiles (ICBMs), although the United States planned to deploy none. However, these asymmetries were also the source of some of the opposition to ratification of the treaty in the U.S. Senate.

It is uncertain how the Soviet decisionmaking process for arms control operates. Most U.S. experts believe that the Soviet military plays the dominant role in deciding on limitations of arms. However, the foreign office, according to some observers, has played a larger role since former Foreign Minister Andrei Gromyko entered the Politburo. It is widely agreed that Soviet negotiators have little, if any, latitude to negotiate. This is often true of U.S. negotiators as well, but most experts agree that Soviet negotiators are generally on a tighter leash. For example, Ambassador U. Alexis Johnson, former head of the U.S. SALT delegation, noted that the Soviets require a consensus within their delegation even on minor points.

The Soviets are tenacious negotiators and attempt to place the burden for compromise on the other side. They negotiate as though they expect a concession for every concession that they make, and tend to keep score based on the number of concessions made by each side, rather than on the relative importance of those concessions. Ambassador Paul Warnke, who served simultaneously as the chief SALT negotiator and director of the Arms Control and Disarmament Agency, believes the Soviet system is not geared for compromise or "splitting differences." While the Soviets have used a refusal to compromise as a negotiating tactic, Herbert York, former U.S. ambassador to the Comprehensive Test Ban negotiations, pointed out that such Soviet intransigence can also reflect an assessment that the United States is not serious about negotiation. A walkout from negotiations, as the Soviets staged in INF and START at the end of 1983, is intended to emphasize the same point. Nevertheless, Soviet negotiators do understand the need to compromise in order to reach agreement, and they will compromise when agreement is important to the Soviet state, as they did in SALT I and II. Indeed, on some occasions the Soviets have shown less reluctance than the Americans to make radical changes in their position. During the 1960s, for instance, they initially opposed limits on ABM, but subsequently, in the SALT talks, they insisted on them.

It is important for U.S. negotiators to assess accurately when the Soviets want agreement and when they just want to discuss arms control issues in some forum. Experienced negotiators such as Paul Warnke have suggested that when Soviet representatives at the table have run out of latitude to negotiate, it is necessary to "drive them back to Moscow" or wait them out. Others have further suggested that when the Soviets are not ready to review their positions — which they do only periodically — it is unproductive for the United States to offer compromises and concessions.[5]

The Soviets prepare very carefully for negotiations (including thorough study of the U.S. negotiators, whom they often try to match

5. Paul H. Nitze, "Living with the Soviets," *Foreign Affairs,* Vol. 63 no. 2 (Winter 1984–85): 360–74.

with a Soviet of equal status), and they usually appear to have very clear objectives in mind. However, the Soviets are not "supermen" when it comes to negotiating. They make their mistakes, just as we do. For example, it now seems that they misjudged Western determination to follow through on INF deployments in 1983 and thus created circumstances that led them to an embarrassing political defeat in Europe.

Individual Soviet negotiators do have different styles. This fact can affect how negotiations are conducted. Several U.S. negotiators commented on the differences, for example, between Vladimir Semenov, the Soviet negotiator in SALT who showed almost no flexibility in negotiations, and Yuli Kvitsinsky, the principal Soviet INF negotiator who engaged in the famous "walk in the woods" with U.S. Ambassador Paul Nitze. But, despite his inflexibility, Semenov negotiated two SALT agreements, while Kvitsinsky's apparent flexibility resulted in a rebuff of his explorations by Moscow. York has suggested that any expression of personal views by a Soviet negotiator should usually be seen as a gambit to elicit a compromise. While major decisions on negotiating positions are made in Moscow and Washington, pressures from the negotiators can often influence decisions in capitals.

The concept of "the spirit of the agreement" has no place in the Soviet approach to arms control. Although Soviet negotiators have no hesitation to employ the concept as a negotiating tactic, Soviet leaders have not acted as though they consider themselves bound to comply beyond the strictest terms of any agreement. We cannot expect that the Soviets will comply with our own interpretation of any concept so vague as an agreement's "spirit." Thus, the United States must ensure that any important provision of an agreement is in writing and that its precise meaning is confirmed by both sides. We must, at least, understand their interpretation and lock that interpretation into the accord.

The Soviets usually look to the United States to make the first concrete proposal. Soviet negotiators prefer to respond rather than initiate but will often react to U.S. positions with detailed proposals of their own. This has been the pattern in SALT I and II and, for the most part, in MBFR (where the Soviets led off with a draft agreement but otherwise responded to NATO initiatives). The United States also was the first party to make detailed proposals in the START and INF negotiations. However, while they do respond, the Soviets are often slow to react to U.S. initiatives. Some cited this delay as a negotiating tactic. Others saw the delay as a reflection of the Soviet decisionmaking process, which often takes a long time to arrive at decisions. Sonnenfeldt commented that it often takes time to convince the Soviets to compromise. Former Ambassador to the MBFR talks Jonathan Dean and others noted that the Soviets seldom change their positions during a negotiating session and only after consultations in Moscow.

The Soviets use numerous negotiating channels. This is, in part, a reflection of the fact that the Soviets view arms control negotiations as part of a broader process designed to protect and promote Soviet security interests. A particularly important channel for the Soviets has been their embassy in Washington. During SALT I and II, for example, Ambassador Anatoliy Dobrynin frequently dealt directly with the secretary of state and the White House. U.S. ambassadors in Moscow—and there have been seven during Ambassador Dobrynin's twenty-three-year tenure in Washington—have never had similar access to senior Soviet officials. This asymmetry was a subject of discussion in the seminars. Some participants suggested that the United States should search for effective methods of insisting on equal treatment for its ambassador in Moscow. Others, while acknowledging the desirability of equal treatment, argued that this was unlikely to prove practical in the foreseeable future.

Some Lessons for Future U.S. Negotiations

The United States must be patient in negotiating with the Soviets. If the United States wants an agreement badly, it is likely to get a bad agreement. For example, SALT I was brought to a conclusion hastily in order to reach agreement at the 1972 Moscow summit meeting. Some important provisions that were the subject of last minute negotiations (e.g., definition of heavy missiles) were later criticized as unequal in Moscow's favor. This perception of inequality (whether or not correct) led to Senator Henry Jackson's initiative demanding equality in SALT II to counteract a future negotiator's urge for agreement. This legislative provision was one factor that prolonged the SALT II negotiations.

Before entering into formal negotiations with the Soviets, the United States should have objectives that are clear and broadly supported within the administration, among the members of Congress, and by the public at large. Often we have not had clear objectives at the outset of negotiation because reaching such a consensus was difficult. At other times, we have changed our objectives in midstream. While setting formal objectives for a negotiation may seem to be merely academic, the process of doing so often clarifies differences and can reduce the prospect of subsequent misunderstanding and bureaucratic haggling.

It is important in negotiating with the Soviets to specify details, wherever possible, in a formal agreement that both parties sign. The Soviets prefer more general agreements but will accept detailed provisions when their need can be demonstrated. Both sides will be tempted to exploit ambiguities in a completed agreement, but the Soviets succumb to this temptation rather regularly. Thus, it is important to make agreements as free of ambiguities as possible. At a minimum, to avoid later misunderstandings, the Soviet interpretation of key provisions should be known before ratification and should be made a part of the negotiating record.

The president and the secretary of state must be personally involved in important negotiations. They must provide strong leadership, particularly if there is bureaucratic opposition to their objectives. However, it is unrealistic to expect senior officials to be responsible for day-to-day management—even in very important negotiations. One suggestion was to place a senior official in charge of negotiations where close presidential direction would not be realistic. This official would be granted unimpeded access to the Oval Office. Others maintained that this alternative would not be practical. They argued that such an individual operating outside the normal bureaucratic process would probably be ineffective, since the major agencies (State and Defense) would insist on a voice in any major policy decision.

Senior negotiators should be involved in the policy formulation process. Negotiators cannot be effective in devising negotiating strategy if they are left out of major decisions, as occurred with Ambassador Gerard Smith in SALT I. Without very careful coordination, conducting negotiations in two locations on the same subject can lead to misunderstanding and confusion. There was some difference of opinion about whether negotiators always need to be aware of fall-back positions before they are employed. Discussing fall-back positions risks the possibility of leaking our position to the other side. Moreover, knowledge of the fall-back position may increase the prospect that a negotiator will move prematurely to compromise before the Soviet position has been fully explored. Many negotiators believe that the person on the spot should have fairly broad latitude to choose tactics, with policy made in Washington. However, there are likely to be differences over what is "policy" and what are "tactics."

So-called "back channel" negotiations between heads of government or foreign ministers are useful, indeed essential. However, there was not agreement on how extensively they should be used. Many experienced negotiators cautioned that such tactics should be used sparingly, or the authority of negotiators will be undermined. Some observers believe that extensive negotiations away from the table in SALT I, conducted by individuals who did not have specific command of all important details, led to some of the ambiguities in the agreement (e.g., on the definition of heavy missiles).

Informal soundings are an essential part of the negotiating process. But they must be used carefully. There are many instances where these moves have been misunderstood or misinterpreted by the Soviets. One experienced negotiator suggested that the senior negotiator should never conduct informal negotiations but should leave exploratory moves to skilled, trusted subordinates because the Soviets usually treat statements by the delegation head as a formal position. On the other hand, precisely because of the risk that such soundings will be misused, many negotiators prefer to conduct this process themselves.

There are differences about whether setting deadlines helps or hurts U.S. interests in negotiations. Some believe the United States should never negotiate against a deadline. They argue that the result will likely be unsatisfactory due to the pressure to reach agreement, and they cite the SALT I negotiations as an example. Others argue that setting deadlines can be a useful way to force the Soviets to make decisions. This group maintains that deadlines are counterproductive only if they are one-sided. In this view, the best deadlines are those that affect both sides equally. Some believe that if deadlines are not set, agreement will never be reached. For example, Jan Lodal, formerly deputy for program analysis on the NSC staff, suggests that without using major political events (e.g., a summit meeting) to drive a negotiation, it will never progress. Professor William Zartman of the School of Advanced International Studies argued that deadlines are inevitable, so we should learn how to use them.

The BATNA concept—"the best alternative to a negotiated agreement"—appealed to many participants. Professor Roger Fisher of Harvard Law School, who invented the concept, argues that any negotiator is well advised before entering into negotiations to have a clear idea of what the best alternatives are if negotiations prove unsuccessful. Failure to evaluate alternative outcomes can lead either to accepting outcomes that could be better achieved by unilateral action or to rejecting agreements that would be preferable to the outcomes that result without agreement. Some experienced negotiators, while acknowledging the attractiveness of BATNA in theory, argued that the concept would be difficult to apply in practice to arms control negotiations. Often the "best" alternatives to a negotiated agreement are far from clear. At least in the United States, they are likely to be influenced by domestic politics. This is perhaps the greatest dilemma the United States faces in an age in which arms control negotiations have become a political, if not a strategic, imperative.

Multilateral Negotiations

There have been several types of multilateral negotiations. Some, such as INF, while bilateral in a formal sense, actually involve important security interests of close U.S. allies. The INF negotiations required continual, intensive consultation between the United States and its NATO allies, particularly those countries where the missiles were to be deployed. Even in the SALT negotiations there was a good deal of consultation with allies. Their interests were expected to be affected by limits on U.S. strategic forces, by the level of ABM deployments, and, even more directly, by the provisions relating to forward-based systems and the transfer of technology that the Soviets attempted to include.

A second type of multilateral negotiations is between two alliances. The MBFR negotiations, which include several direct participant countries from NATO and the Warsaw Pact, are a good example. The substantial time and effort consumed in the coordination of joint positions by the United States and its allies is characteristic of such negotiations. The Soviets spend less time and have considerably less difficulty in coordinating with their allies because of their more dominant position in the Warsaw Pact — although the process is not effortless. This represents a major asymmetry.

A third type of multilateral negotiations involves neutrals and nonaligned states in addition to the alliance members. One example of such negotiations is the Conference on Disarmament in Europe (CDE), which opened in Stockholm in January 1984 and has thirty-five participants representing most of the nations with forces in Europe. Another is the Conference on Disarmament, which is under United Nations auspices in Geneva and has some forty members from all over the world. These forums, being large and unwieldy, tend to become debating societies. Agreements among the diverse interests represented are extremely difficult to reach and tend towards declarations that reflect lowest-common-denominator outcomes. Coordination among allies tends to be looser than in MBFR, largely because the impact of the issues being discussed on vital security interests is not as great and the need for close coordination of positions is therefore not as urgent.

The Soviet role in multilateral negotiations varies depending on the subject matter. In most cases, U.S. and Soviet interests are opposed, but there are exceptions, like the negotiations intended to avert the proliferation of nuclear weapons. In such cases, U.S. negotiators must coordinate with allies, enlist the support of neutrals, and be responsive to public opinion in the West as well as deal with the bureaucracy at home — a complex and difficult task. Soviet negotiators face some of the same problems. They pay attention to Western opinion and seek to influence it, and they must compete with the West for the often critical support of the neutral and non-aligned nations (a task at which they have had little success at the CSCE or CDE). But domestic opinion is hardly a major factor in the Soviet Union, and their allies are less inclined to challenge Soviet leadership, although Romania, Poland, and others have done so on occasion.

Coalition diplomacy has been surprisingly successful in the West, maintaining consensus on most major negotiations. When consensus holds, as it has in MBFR and, for the most part, in INF, the unity of the Western alliance can be an important asset in negotiations. Moreover, allied consensus has a benefit not found in bilateral U.S.-Soviet negotiations: a shared responsibility, visible to the Western public, for the negotiation's outcome, whatever that may be. This consensus has held even in cases where the allies were not direct parties to the negotiations. Nevertheless, there was a strong feeling among the participants in the seminars that if a negotiation applies to the forces of third parties, those states should participate directly in the talks.

Executive–Legislative Relationships in Negotiations

Congress has a major role to play in negotiations with the Soviets — and that role is changing. The importance of the Senate's role in ratifying arms control treaties was dramatized when it failed to ratify the SALT II agreement in 1979–80. In the last several years, Capitol Hill has become increasingly active in arms control. Congress has passed resolutions supporting the nuclear freeze and, more specifically, initiatives intended to influence executive branch positions in negotiations. For example, in 1984 there was a series of initiatives, notably by Congressman Les Aspin (D.-Wisconsin), that sought to tie funding for MX and other strategic programs to progress in arms control.

Divided authority between the legislative and executive branches in foreign policy has long been a unique feature of the U.S. system. It frequently leads to delay or even impasse in implementing policy, which can be embarrassing for U.S. leadership and confusing to foreigners. This was the case with the U.S. failure to join the League of Nations in the 1920s and, more recently, with the failure to ratify the SALT II Treaty. When there are pressures from Congress to alter negotiating positions or to accelerate the pace of negotiations, as there were during the START and INF negotiations in 1981–83, it becomes difficult to adopt and maintain a firm opening position, even when this may be a desirable negotiating tactic. The Soviets seek to exploit any divisions in the United States, so domestic consensus, at least on the broad objectives of the negotiation, is important to successful negotiations.

Another feature of the U.S. system, different from that of the Soviet Union, is the relatively frequent change of political leadership accompanied by an urge to alter the appearance (if not the substance) of policies, as well as the policymakers themselves. The Soviet bureaucracy and its senior negotiators are a far more stable group than their American counterparts. This phenomenon has a significant impact on arms control. For example, the new strategic arms proposals made by the Carter administration in March 1977 appeared to repudiate the Vladivostok accords negotiated by the prior administration and were rejected immediately by the Soviets. The Reagan administration, in turn, made radical changes in strategic arms proposals, apparently altering many of the ground rules negotiated by the Carter administration and incorporated in the SALT II Treaty, which Reagan had declared to be "fatally flawed" before the 1980 election. Consequently, little progress was made on strategic arms control during the first Reagan administration. In both cases, the new administration eventually ended up accepting, for the most part, the legacy of its predecessor. But these changes in position from one administration to the next, even if only temporary, and the fanfare that accompanies such shifts give the impression that the United States is an erratic and unreliable negotiating partner.

The seminars discussed these issues and possible solutions. No one believed that the U.S. constitutional system was likely to change in the foreseeable future, although some have argued that this change is desirable. For now, the separation of powers is a basic fact. Nor did any participant believe that Congress could be bypassed in any major arms control negotiations by the use of executive agreements.

One way to involve Congress more closely in negotiations and minimize the possibility of a repetition of the SALT II experiences would be to include congressional representatives as part of the negotiating team. U.S. Delegate at Large to the strategic arms talks James Woolsey observed that representatives from the Congress are more likely to be team players when they are seated face-to-face with Soviet negotiators across the table. Some participants favored the inclusion of members of Congress as formal members of the negotiating team; others espoused an advisory role, with "visiting rights" to the negotiating site.

Another suggestion was to keep agreements as simple as possible. Woolsey noted a trend toward proposals that provide flexibility within broad ceilings (e.g., the build-down approach) rather than detailed limits, and thought this might facilitate congressional support. However, others suggested that complexity often arises from the effort to remove ambiguities and to assure verification, which is an important issue with some members of Congress.

Several participants noted that a major obstacle to bipartisanship is a tendency for the public debate on arms control to exaggerate the benefits (or costs) and oversimplify the issues associated with certain approaches such as the freeze. The exploitation of arms control agreements for political purposes by their supporters and critics alike is a bipartisan phenomenon and has proven difficult to curb. It would be highly desirable to reduce exaggerated public expectations for arms control, but this may prove very difficult. In sum, there was broad agreement that bipartisanship in dealing with the Soviets was highly desirable, but that politicization of arms control was becoming more, not less, prevalent. This is likely to complicate future negotiations and reduce the certainty of ratifying controversial treaties.

Negotiating in the U.S. Bureaucracy

A number of former U.S. negotiators observed that arms control negotiations with the Soviet Union are invariably complicated by negotiations within the U.S. bureaucracy. The latter can be more contentious and much more time consuming than U.S.–Soviet talks. Several U.S. government agencies have expertise and interests in arms control negotiations. However, these interests are often not congruent. Differences between the State and Defense Departments over the START and INF negotiations have been reported frequently in the press. As York pointed out, there can be differences even among the military services, as there were in the antisatellite negotiations in 1978–79, in which he was involved.

Policies and specific instructions for arms control negotiations are formulated in interagency committees comprised of representatives of the major concerned agencies. The particular agencies differ depending on the subject of the negotiations, but they invariably include the State and Defense Departments, the National Security Council (NSC), and the Arms Control and Disarmament Agency (ACDA). The interagency process gives officials of each agency a veto, even over quite minute details. As a result, the system tends to move slowly unless there is a strong interest at senior levels to force decisions. On the other hand, the process usually assures that all views are heard, and it may be the only way to ensure broad support for the final positions.

As York has noted, bureaucrats who are opposed to a particular agreement can manipulate the process to delay negotiations. He believes this was done in the case of the comprehensive test ban (CTB) negotiations. He accepted that all interested parties must be included in the discussion and debate over whether to negotiate a particular. agreement. But he argued that, to avoid lengthy delays or actually blocking agreement, once a decision to negotiate is made, opponents of the negotiations must accept that decision and abjure efforts to slow or prevent negotiating progress.

Another solution, suggested by Dean, would be to put a senior official with direct access to the president (probably on the NSC staff), specifically in charge of guiding a negotiation from Washington when the president or the secretary of state cannot devote substantial personal attention to the negotiation. Others in the seminars expressed the view that such an approach was unlikely to be effective because arms control frequently involves sensitive security issues, and there are real differences of view about how to resolve them. Furthermore, agreement will not always be the objective, in which case there would be no need for special arrangements to expedite agreement. Several participants, including both former Deputy Under Secretary of State for Security Assistance, Science, and Technology Joseph Nye, who was involved with nonproliferation talks, and Sonnenfeldt, pointed out that reaching an agreement is not always — or at least should not be — the prime U.S. objective. Some participants contended that any special provisions designed to accelerate the pace of negotiations and override bureaucratic obstacles would be appropriate only if there were a presidential decision that reaching agreement was an urgent priority. In that case, it should be relatively easy to overcome bureaucratic obstacles.

2 SOVIET NEGOTIATING CONCEPT AND STYLE

Helmut Sonnenfeldt

This chapter discusses Soviet negotiating concept and style and suggests lessons U.S. negotiators can learn from previous experience in negotiating with the Soviets. It covers four areas concerning Soviet negotiating: some aspects of Soviet foreign policy—the context of Soviet negotiating, the Soviet concept of negotiations, the Soviet negotiating style, and a comparison of Soviet diplomatic style with that of the United States and its allies. The chapter concludes with lessons for negotiators.

SOVIET FOREIGN POLICY AS A CONTEXT FOR SOVIET NEGOTIATING

The work of diplomacy—that which occurs in the Foreign Ministry, embassies, and international organizations—is only one component in Soviet foreign policy. The two other key components are the Soviet drive for power and influence in the world, much of which is based on their military power, and the continuing heritage of Soviet ideology, their outlook on the world.

This combination of foreign policy tools has produced some successes for Soviet foreign policy, such as the control of threats on Soviet borders. But there have also been cases where the components of Soviet foreign policy contradicted one another, contributing to failures. Soviet aggression in the 1940s and 1950s was one reason for the formation of the Western alliance, which clearly ran counter to the Soviet interest of dividing Western Europe and the United States. More recently, the Soviet effort combining negotiation with the United States, agitation and diplomatic pressure in Western Europe, and the deployment of modernized shorter-range missiles failed to prevent the beginning of the deployment of the U.S. intermediate-range nuclear missiles in Europe designed to counter the SS–20. There have also been cases where KGB activities interfered with other efforts to court potentially friendly countries.

In terms of the international role of the Soviet Union, forces are pulling the Soviets in two directions — one toward more involvement in the international system and one toward more isolation. Notwithstanding the peculiarities that make the Soviet Union a special case in the world of diplomacy, the reality of today's interrelated world has forced the Soviets to become involved. They see benefits to be gained in areas of economics and in the regimes of the oceans and the skies. They also have grudgingly come to accept that international involvement is necessary because there are conditions that affect them, such as the world economy and the environment, that they do not control. Accordingly, the Soviet Union now has a greater and more widespread reliance on the external world than it initially had, particularly under Stalin.

Furthermore, the Soviets have adjusted their compulsive secrecy to some extent as a result of improvements in the technology that permits us to penetrate that secrecy, such as satellite reconnaissance. For example, they have grown more willing to provide us in arms control negotiations with information on their military forces, realizing that we can obtain much information through surveillance, anyway.[1]

However, the Soviet regime is quite ambivalent about this trend toward increased world involvement. They place great stock in maintaining the isolation of their political and economic system and their population, believing that acceptance of Western notions of inter-

---

1. A participant in the seminars cited some evidence for this evolution. In SALT I, Soviet military representatives asked the United States to discontinue the practice of bringing up data about Soviet military forces in the talks because they did not want their civilian colleagues to get the information. In SALT II, a shift in this habit of secrecy was signified by the formal Soviet submission of data on their strategic forces for the first time.

dependence could undermine their monopoly of power. They are sensitive and suspicious about any negotiation with the outside world. As a result, in negotiations entailing a high degree of interaction, we are bound to encounter great resistance to efforts to penetrate Soviet secrecy. The Soviets are generally restrictive and legalistic about any form of intrusion. This is true in arms control talks, particularly when we seek more than external means of observing Soviet compliance, such as on-site inspection. It is also true in cultural exchanges when foreign contacts are involved, in economic and commercial agreements when disclosure of data is requested, and in international organizations when disclosure of information is required.

This impulse toward secrecy is strengthened by the Soviet awareness of their self-isolation. The Soviets still have an enormous sense of particularity about themselves and are fundamentally very isolated, in some respects self-isolated. They have no real friends in the world, only temporary friends, prudential friends. In some ways they are the most unloved government and perhaps most seriously unloved in what they think of as their own camp.

The forces pulling the Soviets into the international community provide a challenge for U.S. policy and that of the outside world; namely, to persuade the Soviets to accept the disciplines and constraints, as well as the benefits, of world involvement. We need to make them recognize that seeking the benefits of world involvement is not compatible with throwing their weight around.

Despite increasing Soviet international involvement, the current generation of Soviet leadership has had little exposure to the outside world. The late Soviet President Leonid Brezhnev and Foreign Minister Andrei Gromyko are exceptions to this rule, having had extensive contacts with foreign leaders. Beyond the leadership, Soviet diplomats, who represent Soviet foreign policy to the world and many of whom comprise Soviet negotiating teams, are quite professional and knowledgeable about their areas of specialty. They probably have as solid and intensive a training as diplomats of other countries and are more specialized. However, the high degree of compartmentalization of information in the Soviet system renders Soviet diplomats less well-informed about a range of issues and even about matters concerning their own country than are Western diplomats. Soviet negotiators are carefully instructed but are not necessarily very knowledgeable about the broad underlying considerations and strategy pertaining to their negotiations.

THE SOVIET CONCEPT OF NEGOTIATIONS

The Soviets have a broad conception of what constitutes negotiations. They see negotiations, particularly those on arms control, as part of a broader security effort designed to prevent the coalescence of forces hostile to them. They are generally serious about negotiations, but they resort to extraneous elements and extra-negotiating techniques beyond the negotiating table to get support for their position. These outside influences can be of considerable importance in Soviet negotiating policy. For the Soviets, negotiations do not mean simply sitting down and haggling over language at the bargaining table, but rather maneuvering for position and achieving certain adjustments by one means or another, including the threat of force, agitation, bribery, and other inducements.

Traditionally, the Soviets have not been as much concerned about concluding an agreement in negotiations as about using the process to promote their own interests. Americans often feel uneasy if a negotiation does not conclude with a completed document, signed, sealed, and delivered. This is not the case with the Soviets. They have often been prepared to engage in endless talk and negotiations without conclusion and still attempt to promote their interests through that process.

The Soviets, therefore, value negotiations. In the last 20 to 25 years, they have conducted negotiations on a wide range of issues where they want to protect and advance their interests — arms control, political matters, and economic areas. They do not want agreements at any price. They always have a very steep price. In any case, the Soviets see virtue in negotiations and have long since overcome whatever inhibitions they once had about signing agreements or completing agreements with class adversaries. So the Soviets must be treated as serious negotiators.

THE SOVIET NEGOTIATING STYLE

The Soviets deserve respect as negotiators, but they are not, as some would have us believe, infallible "super negotiators" who get their way in every case through tenacity, trickery, shrewdness, or superior knowledge. There is a kind of mystique that the Soviets out-bargain everybody. I do not think that is true.[2]

As negotiators, the Soviets are tenacious. Usually, they begin a negotiation by taking a very firm position and putting the burden of compromise on the other side, though they endeavor to put a reasonable face on their position. The negotiators say, in effect, "This is our position; of course, we are willing to hear yours," and so on. They do tend to convey the impression that they have a really firm position. But, from all the negotiations in which I have been involved, it is clear that the initial Soviet position was not the final position, that there is give, though certainly within limits, and that when they want an agreement they understand that it requires compromise. The extent of compromise, however, depends upon the negotiating skill of the other side, on what might be called "the objective surrounding circumstances," and on how much incentive the Soviets have — or think they have — to come to terms.

Soviet negotiators yield points rather grudgingly, and in yielding, resort to a tactic of dramatizing their concession. They use their own readiness to compromise on a particular point to extract a greater compromise from the other side in return. They expect gratitude for what they have done. Frequently, Soviet negotiators will yield on a point that should not have been held for so long a time. But once they start adjusting, they always seem to be in a great hurry to wrap things up. One must be careful not to be caught up in a spiral of euphoria and gratitude toward the Soviets.

Deadlines, such as summits or treaty expirations, can influence negotiations. The Soviets will not concede on something they value enormously in these situations, but deadlines can help the other side win on some points. For example, the Soviets wanted to create the impression of success at the 1972 U.S.-Soviet summit and may have given up more on the SALT agreements and the pact on incidents at sea than they would have without the deadline imposed by the summit. Sometimes the Soviets have simply made a decision on a negotiation and want an agreement quickly. In these instances, as in the case of the Austrian State Treaty of 1955, a skillful negotiator can extract Soviet concessions.

---

2. Another participant added that, in his view, we not only overrate Soviet negotiating abilities but also underrate our own.

COMPARISON OF NEGOTIATING STYLES

Changes in Soviet negotiating behavior since the days of the cold war raise a basic question about the possible convergence of diplomatic styles. A certain "normal behavior" has been discernible in the conduct of Soviet negotiators, normal in the sense that negotiators are engaged in a time-honored practice for which there are certain ground rules that have long been established in international custom. The Soviets, having started in 1917 by putting themselves outside of the conventional international system, have had to return to that system and adapt themselves to many of its practices. In short, the Soviets have accommodated to the stylistic requirements of diplomacy and negotiations in contemporary international relations.

But there is a difference between the American experience in negotiating with its allies and with the Soviets. In negotiating with the Soviets, one never has the sense of a degree of comity or commonality of approach. There is always a strong residue of antagonism indicating that, by and large, negotiations with the Soviets are adversary proceedings. That is not to say that negotiations with friends are not also adversary proceedings. Even then the two sides have conflicting interests on economic and other matters. But the allies share an overarching belief in common values, a belief that the Soviets lack.

Another difference between U.S. and Soviet styles is that the Americans tend to negotiate in behalf of broad and universalist objectives such as stability, while the Soviets are concerned essentially with their own national security. They will not permit arms control agreements to limit significantly their military programs but invariably seek to have agreements limit, to the greatest extent possible, U.S. defense programs that concern them. The United States, of course, also seeks to limit disturbing Soviet programs. However, there is an asymmetry in that the Soviets have no one in their policymaking apparatus trying to use arms control to limit their own programs, while the United States does have such influences.

Americans and Soviets do have certain common concerns not shared by other nations. Control of the vast machinery of destruction, the fear of war, and concern about the responsibility of preventing horrible wars perhaps unite us with the Soviets even more than with our closest friends because we have looked into the abyss together. To some extent, this is evident in U.S.–Soviet discussions about crises or problems of the world order at arms control talks or at the summit level. One cannot help but have the sense in these settings that here are representatives of two countries who do, in many ways, hold the peace of the world and the future of mankind in their hands. Furthermore, in some specific instances, U.S. and Soviet mutual interests permit agreements that serve these interests very well in practice. Two such cases are the Nuclear Non-Proliferation Treaty and the Antarctic Treaty.

However, I would caution against exaggerating the degree of commonality that this shared relationship yields because the relationship remains an adversarial one. Sometimes this problem of responsibility for the peace of the world acquires the characteristic of a tough game of "chicken." Who can be pushed the furthest given the fear of cataclysmic war? Moreover, while fear of a nuclear war helps to sustain nuclear arms talks, it has not produced effective mechanisms to reduce the risk of war, as distinct from the efforts to defuse crises that have occurred in such situations as the 1962 Cuban missile crisis and the 1973 Yom Kippur War.

Thus, while there is something to the notion of a common sense of responsibility, it ought not be carried too far, for it does not outweigh the relationship's many aspects that remain highly antagonistic and that involve quite different values and outlooks on the world.

LESSONS LEARNED FROM SOVIET NEGOTIATING BEHAVIOR

U.S.–Soviet negotiations are a special situation, though not so special that we can lose sight of some of the general rules of negotiations. These include being clear about our objectives, precise and concrete in our proposals, flexible in response to the other side's proposals, and patient, as well as having an understanding of and regard for the interests and sensitivities of the other side. The calculation of how our interests are best served is really more important than the skill of our negotiators. Also, we should avoid the assumption that a negotiation must produce an agreement in order to be successful. It may be just as valuable to provide a means of communication in order to convey ideas and attitudes.

On the other hand, we must recognize that the Soviets represent, if not a unique problem, then certainly a very special one for us. They have a hostile and suspicious view of the outside world, particularly of the United States as the other superpower and, in their view, the principal opponent of their ambitions. The Soviets have a style of negotiation that can be excruciatingly pedantic and slow in an effort to wait out their bargaining opponent. They rely more than most countries on outside pressures to influence negotiations. This is particularly so in arms control talks, for which they attempt to mobilize threats and inducements such as the activities of mass movements and other communist parties. The Soviet negotiator is really a point man for a whole panoply of strategies and tactics. Finally, the Soviets see negotiations as not necessarily leading to formal agreement but as a form of manipulation and pressures.

Thus, dealing with the Soviets is a special situation that stems from the particular type of people that the Soviets are, including their psychological make-up and ideological baggage, and the type of people that we are. But we must be careful not to become overly entranced with broad prescriptions and simple theories about how the Soviets negotiate. Some recurring patterns do obviously exist. But there is also a strong personal element in the formal negotiating process. Above all, the important thing to remember is that negotiation in the strict sense of the term—diplomatic exchange, bargaining, the effort to achieve documents constituting agreement—is only a portion of the continuous process of negotiation in the broader sense.

We must be patient in negotiating with the Soviets. How long we can wait for them to change a position depends on how interested we are in an agreement. They will, of course, attempt to maximize their interests. For example, in arms talks they will often attempt to slow or stop our defense programs. But they do recognize that in negotiating security there must be reciprocal benefits, and there is flexibility in their approach. It takes time to convince the Soviets to compromise, and thus there is considerable virtue in a good deal of patience. Sometimes standing pat in negotiations will enable us to win concessions, though probably not on major issues. In some cases, particularly when the Soviets appear to need an agreement, it may be best to go without one for a time and wait for them to offer a more forthcoming position.

We must be ready to go beyond the negotiating table and bring external pressures to bear. It is not possible to state general rules for applying such pressures to obtain negotiating leverage. But we should be skillful and subtle enough to take advantage of them when possible.

The Soviet need for healthy economic relations with the West serves as one means of leverage in our negotiations. We cannot expect to eliminate entirely the antagonism and maneuvering for geopolitical advantage that characterizes U.S.-Soviet relations. We can, however, demonstrate to the Soviets that growth in the scope and intensity of economic relations must be compatible with growth in scope and intensity of political relations. Thus, an East-West relationship of restraint should be a condition for large-scale economic relations. This approach has worked in East Germany, where the Soviet Union has permitted increased contacts with the West so that East Germany can acquire loans from West Germany.

Such restraint will make the political atmosphere more conducive to negotiations, and the Soviets' desire for commerce might make them more forthcoming in political and arms control dealings. However, we should realize that economic carrots and sticks will not significantly change Soviet actions when vital interests are at stake, as they were in Poland in 1981. In that case, the prospect of a renewed U.S. grain embargo may have caused the Soviets to resort to different means (persuading the Polish government to impose martial law, rather than invading Poland themselves), though they did ultimately achieve their objective of crushing Poland's free trade union movement. What we can do is use incentives and sanctions to induce more and more restraint over time, particularly in areas more remote from and of less vital interest to the Soviet Union.

Arms control negotiations are particularly subject to the impact of other international events. For example, the opening of the SALT I talks was postponed by the Soviet intervention in Czechoslovakia, and the SALT II talks were greatly influenced by Soviet actions in East Africa and Afghanistan. We should continue to link arms control negotiations to Soviet international activities as another means of inducing Soviet restraint. But such negotiations probably have little tactical bargaining value in regard to specific political problems. Moreover, we have reservations about linkage on our side, since there are strong pressures on U.S. administrations to engage in arms talks.

Finally, the success of cooperation in areas of mutual interest is dependent on the maintenance of a properly balanced power relationship. In the SALT negotiations, for example, the military balance — actual and prospective — was an extremely important factor. This does not argue for assuming bargaining chip positions, however. It is unwise to develop and buy expensive forces simply for the sake of trading them away again on the bargaining table.[3] Forces should be bought to serve requirements, and they should be maintained as long as they are needed. If negotiations or unilateral actions remove or reduce a requirement, then the forces designed to meet it can be adjusted accordingly. In practice, however, arms control negotiations have done little to change previously planned military programs.

We should be knowledgeable in the subject matter being negotiated, not only in its narrow sense but also in its relationship to the broader scheme of things. This requires being meticulous in negotiations without being too legalistic, a fault that sometimes impairs us.

The scope of formal agreements with the Soviet Union should be narrow and definable. However, we should recognize that the narrower the scope of an arms control agreement, the more likely the Soviets will compensate with means that are not limited, as has been the case on both sides with underground nuclear testing since the Limited Test Ban Treaty. Agreements should be as detailed as possible in order to minimize misunderstandings and loopholes. Experience has proven that the Soviets are good at discovering loopholes. Occasionally, a joint declaration of intent that is not very precise can be useful, but it can also lead to more, rather than less, friction, as happened with the 1972 Statement of Agreed Principles and the 1973 Agreement on the Prevention of Nuclear War.

We should beware of elaborate, comprehensive arms control agreements. They can take so long to negotiate as to lose much relevance by the time they are concluded. In general, we should adhere to the "pothole theory" of arms control, which draws an analogy with the notion that, while a large metropolis may be ultimately ungovernable, at least the potholes can be filled: While extensive arms control agreements may be unmanageable, small security problems can be solved with limited agreements.

We should keep in mind three key points regarding the negotiating team. First, it is necessary to involve responsible senior negotiators in

3. The question of bargaining chips elicited several comments. One participant drew a distinction between two kinds of bargaining chips—those which constitute threats and those which are warnings. The former would actually hurt our position, though it would hurt the other side's position more. The latter would be an overall benefit to us. In general, he argued, warnings are useful bargaining chips, whereas threats are not. Another speaker said we should beware of bargaining chips that commit us with weapons we do not necessarily want or need. A third suggested that weapon systems on which there is substantial disagreement tend to become bargaining chips.

the policymaking process, notwithstanding the value of sometimes keeping the negotiator unaware of his fall-back positions. Because of our open political system, negotiators cannot be isolated from policy development. They are accountable to Congress and the public and thus must be kept reasonably well informed. The involvement of a senior official in Washington or another Western capital can occasionally enable previously unattainable progress at the negotiating table. Although in the Nixon administration it was possible to conclude desirable agreements without our formal negotiators being fully informed, as a general rule it is best for the senior negotiators to know about such contacts and be involved in policymaking.[4]

Having said that, however, the second point is that "back channel" communications are a necessary part of negotiating. Inevitably, there will be several levels of discourse and bargaining, and sometimes the information cannot be made available to all involved in negotiations because of its extreme sensitivity. Ideally, the different modes of communication — the various "channels" — should be in harmony. But I think it is wrong to argue that every official is entitled to know about every communication that passes between heads of government.[5]

Furthermore, while there are hazards in back channel communications, it is an invalid criticism to suggest that a head of state or senior official should be barred from communicating in special ways with his counterpart. It is certainly a president's prerogative to determine his own role in a negotiation, depending on his judgment of how that role may complicate the formulation of policy for the negotiation.

Third, informal contacts between members of negotiating teams are valuable in probing the Soviet position and providing insight on possible infighting among their policymakers. However, these contacts

4. Several participants agreed that a good rule of thumb was that policy should be determined in Washington with the involvement of the head of delegation, while the delegation should be permitted to work out its own tactics.

5. The back channel issue has been particularly controversial since SALT I, and this was reflected in the discussion. Some participants felt that the SALT I delegation had been undermined by contacts between Moscow and Washington of which they were unaware. Some, though they did accept the need for such contacts, also argued that the chief negotiator should be informed of all back channel conversations.

There was further discussion on the general subject of contacts between U.S. and Soviet officials. One speaker pushed for increased use of the U.S. Embassy in Moscow to communicate with the Soviets, as well as multiple channels of continuing professional, including military-to-military, contacts. He argued these channels would help us penetrate the Soviet facade. Another replied that Soviet leaders would not let us use the embassy more because they like to keep a buffer of lower officials between themselves and U.S. representatives. A third suggested that communication might be improved if we made our heads of delegations Soviet experts.

must avoid the impression that firm positions are being stated or that the Soviets can exploit our own internal disagreements. Also, they should be reported faithfully and promptly so that they can be assessed by someone with a broader perspective on the negotiations. Soviet negotiators in arms and even economic talks may not be as fully informed on issues related to the talks as U.S. negotiators, but their comments in informal talks can still be useful.

We should be cautious and sparing in using private groups or individuals who visit the Soviet Union as semi-official representatives of the U.S. government. There is a sizable number of Americans who talk to Soviets regularly as private citizens. This dialogue can have some impact on Soviet perceptions of American policy and of the degree of political support for or opposition to it. Some American private citizens participate in government-sponsored research or in government panels and commissions, through which the Soviets can gain insights into internal American debates. But generally it does not benefit the U.S. government to use such individuals to carry formal messages, since this confuses what should remain a reasonably clear distinction between official representatives and private persons. Apart from trying to gain insights from private groups, the Soviets also use them as "conveyor belts" for what they want the American government to know or for influencing U.S. policy debates. Thus, U.S. government involvement with private groups should be handled with great care.

The backstopping process works best when there is strong central guidance for the negotiations. With strong guidance, including a good chairman—usually the White House or NSC—backstopping can keep negotiations on track and provide the negotiating team with expeditious and coordinated instructions. Without strong guidance, interagency battles are likely to become debilitating, and instructions to delegations may degenerate to a lowest common denominator and thus prove unhelpful. The nature of the backstopping process will vary from administration to administration. The key to its effectiveness is not the process itself but the strength of leadership provided to it.

Ultimately, negotiating with the Soviets, broadly construed as how we defend and advance our interests vis-à-vis the Soviet Union, is crucial because it significantly affects our security and well-being and questions of war and peace. Only a small part of negotiations in the broadest sense takes place at a negotiating table, but we should treat every encounter seriously and handle it meticulously. This will assure that the Soviets will take us seriously at the bargaining table.

3 SOVIET NEGOTIATING PRACTICE

Sidney N. Graybeal

This chapter examines the Soviet negotiating process as distinct from the substance of negotiations. The observations herein on composition of the delegations, negotiating formats and types of meetings, tactics, and problems with the resulting agreements are drawn from lessons learned through personal experience.

THE COMPOSITION OF DELEGATIONS

Soviet negotiating teams are comprised of veterans and professionals. The Soviets maintain continuity within the delegation. On the other hand, the United States tends to make numerous changes at all levels. Some argue that it is advantageous to have a more experienced delegation; others note the merits of rotating membership and of injecting new blood. The Soviets appear to believe that experience and continuity are the most important factors. On the American side, some consider it dangerous to allow people to remain on the delegation for too long, fearing that such negotiators come to believe too strongly in the agreement they are pursuing and may seek agreement for agreement's sake.

The Soviet choice of the delegation head often signals who is in charge in Moscow. It also signals the nature and type of negotiation. In the case of the Standing Consultative Commission (SCC), Georgiy Ivanovich Ustinov, a two-star general, was made the first Soviet commissioner. His deputy was Victor Karpov, who was Ambassador Rowny's counterpart in the START talks of 1982–83. Karpov outranked Ustinov in terms of the overall hierarchy, but the Soviets put a military man in charge of implementing agreements that deal with military systems. The United States did just the opposite. We appointed a civilian commissioner and a military deputy.

It is telling to note who is present when the negotiations commence, as well as the balance within the delegation between military, civilian, and scientific experts. For example, for the Surprise Attack Conference, the U.S. team underwent three weeks of intensive preparations. Our delegation included one four-star general, three three-star generals, and twelve top scientists versed in radar, seismology, weapons, and other technical subjects. The Soviet delegation was composed of representatives of the Ministry of Foreign Affairs and a few military personnel. When we asked where their technical experts were, they replied that they were in Moscow and would be called when needed. This was a clear signal that the Soviets wanted to discuss the agenda and general scope of the negotiations, not the subject itself. And that is just what happened. For two weeks we argued about the agenda and never reached agreement. The conference was recessed eight weeks later and is still in recess. Anyone worried about surprise attack might consider reconvening that conference.

The Soviets generally appoint a delegation head and delegates with the same general ranks as their U.S. counterparts. They are very conscious of position, experience, and age. They want to be treated as equals and usually seek comparability in each of the relevant positions. Moreover, Soviet delegates know their counterparts. They have excellent biographic information and study it thoroughly before coming to a session. Note their questions and comments. The delegates may be able tell you more about yourself than you have told them. They will also explore for additional details to augment their biographic information. This is part of their job, and they usually do it better than most U.S. delegates.

The Soviets manifest a complete consistency of positions at all levels and in various private exchanges. Their well-orchestrated game plan is evident both in their plenary statement and in private conversations between heads of delegations, delegates, and advisers.[1] The delegates sometimes try the gambit of playing off their military members against their political or foreign affairs members. For example, the political people may claim that they are having difficulty getting the military to agree to a U.S. proposal. "If the United States would just make these changes," they say, "we could probably persuade the military to acquiesce." One should take most of these gambits for what they are, not for actual divisiveness.

In negotiations with the Soviets, heads of delegations cannot have unofficial exchanges. Advisers can be used for exploratory activities because they are expendable. But the head of a delegation is not expendable and should not explore beyond his instructions. Anything he says or does is an official statement.

Each delegation includes qualified interpreters. It is imperative to use interpreters for all official discussions. Interpreters are even more valuable if they participate in preparations for a meeting, so that they know exactly what meaning to attach to a particular English word. There may be more than one Soviet word to translate a given English word. In the case of the SCC, the interpreter attended our planning sessions so he knew exactly what the head of the delegation wished to communicate. If he had a choice of words, he could question which was the best.

During the Anti-Ballistic Missile (ABM) Treaty negotiations, I headed a working group with Karpov as my counterpart to refine the language of some of the articles of the ABM Treaty that had been agreed upon in principle at the higher level. We were not making much progress on one article. Karpov loves to needle, and, although he speaks English, he made a statement in Russian because some of his members did not understand English. Translating, the interpreter said, "Well, Mr. Graybeal, if you do not have the competence..." At that point Karpov interrupted and corrected, "authority, authority." Apparently, the Soviet word for the two is very similar. The interpreter used the word "competence," which inferred something personal. But Karpov just wanted to needle me by pointing out that my

---

1. A participant who had headed a U.S. delegation to important U.S.–Soviet talks added that his Soviet counterpart apparently had to get a consensus within his delegation before making decisions on negotiating tactics.

government did not grant me the authority to settle a particular issue, whereas his government did grant him that authority.

Now, Karpov corrected that mistake. But imagine a kitchen conversation between Brezhnev and Nixon, where only a Soviet interpreter is present. Suppose Brezhnev makes a comparable statement to Nixon, and it is translated as "competence" instead of "authority". Insofar as Nixon and Brezhnev do not understand each other's language, such a mistake could create a serious problem. This is just one example of the vital role an interpreter can play in the negotiating process.

Keep in mind that all Soviet delegations include one or more KGB officers. They are usually listed as interpreters or advisers, but they can usually be identified early in the exchanges. Frequently, CIA biographic data provides a fairly thorough account of the composition of the Soviet delegation. One should not be overly concerned about a delegation's KGB members. Nor, on the other hand, should one try to outmaneuver them. They generally have greater expertise in that sort of thing than most U.S. delegates.

NEGOTIATING FORMATS

In the arms control process, there are usually some formal plenary meetings. These include an exchange of statements and possibly some dialogue. The extent of dialogue depends on the head of the delegation and his willingness to engage in across-the-table exchanges. Aside from plenaries, there are also mini-plenaries; in the case of SALT, there were "troikas" and working groups. These are somewhat formal in nature, and may or may not include exchanges of papers; they usually include dialogue across the table. In addition, there are private exchanges at all levels. The most important of these occur between heads of delegations and are generally very formal. The head of the Soviet SALT I delegation, Vladimir Semenov, usually had talking points and normally did not pass them to his counterpart. He seldom deviated from his talking points; hence, there was often very little constructive dialogue.

Delegation advisers can be vital in probing the Soviets for possible fall-back positions. But remember that the Soviets are also probing our side, so advisers should not be given too much latitude in providing indications of U.S. fall-back positions. Executive officers can be useful for both substantive activities and administration. Dr. Raymond Garthoff and I worked as a team in SALT I. He was the executive officer; I was his alternate. He handled the substantive exploration; I handled administration, tactics, and preparation of statements. The executive officer can play a key role. In the SCC, he was highly valuable in acquiring information about Soviet approaches. Interpreters are also extremely useful in talking to counterparts about precisely what meaning they attach to a particular Soviet word.

It is important to maintain privacy in negotiations. This indicates the seriousness of the negotiations. It also provides the opportunity for making constructive progress. In arms control, one is often negotiating in a fishbowl. With allies, the public, and Congress looking over one's shoulder, it can be a very difficult process. Congress can and should be involved, but in a way that maintains as much privacy as is possible in our society. Privacy will also help avoid polemics. The Soviets often make statements in an open negotiating context that are intended for consumption by a broader audience. This is a problem in the United Nations Conference on Disarmament (CD), the Eighteen Nation Disarmament Conference (ENDC), and other multinational forums where the Soviets know they will be heard by parties in addition to the United States.

The Soviets are quite conscious of protocol. They are sensitive to any change in established procedures, even minor ones such as a change in location. One day in the SCC, it was inconvenient to use our Mission conference room in Geneva. So, I asked the executive officer to change the meeting. That meant meeting at the Soviet Mission twice in a row. Immediately they were suspect. "What is Graybeal up to? Normally the guest speaks first. Does he want to get something on the table before we have a chance to speak?" In general, the Soviets are very suspicious people and will often attribute to us the worst of motives.

The Soviets view personal relationships, as well as private dinners, lunches, and meetings, as important opportunities for doing business. On such occasions they size up their counterparts and attempt to probe for fallback positions and weaknesses. It is difficult to have a truly informal lunch, dinner, or meeting, particularly for a head of a delegation or a senior delegate or adviser. One can be sure that one's comments and views will be recorded and recalled at subsequent, opportune moments. U.S. delegates should avoid toasting and drinking contests with their Soviet counterparts. Our side inevitably loses.

One must assume that any exchange in a Soviet-controlled facility will be monitored. This is a problem when negotiating in Moscow or at the Soviet Embassy or Mission. If there is a need to call the delegation together to resolve an issue, and if the Soviets offer the use of a "private room" to do so, it is best to refuse and postpone the issue until it can be resolved on home turf. Likewise, if we offer the Soviets a private room in an American facility, they will suspect that the room is monitored.

NEGOTIATING TACTICS

The Soviets come to the bargaining table extremely well prepared. They know what their ultimate goals are and keep them constantly in mind. Typically, at the start of a negotiation, the Soviets will have devised a game plan and associated tactics for at least the first four or five plenary meetings. They hate for events to divert them from that game plan. They abhor agenda changes. They want to know the agenda in advance whenever possible. Knowing the agenda enables them to be prepared, to coordinate their positions in Moscow, and to get advice. The Soviets do not like surprises. They constantly endeavor to determine the U.S. fall-back position at all levels.

Soviet delegations have little authority to make spot decisions, particularly on items beyond their specific guidance. They must check with Moscow on all points, major or minor, before overstepping their instructions. Ironically, they are extremely reluctant to check back home because they feel it reflects poorly on their capabilities. Nevertheless, they are very careful to avoid antagonizing the home office. Note that, in many cases, checking with Moscow takes time. Also, delays are longer around official Soviet holidays such as the new year, May Day, or October Revolution Day.[2]

The Soviets generally prefer that the United States take the initiative in proposing solutions to controversial points. They maintain that it is easier for Moscow to react than to act. (Most heads of U.S.

2. One participant suggested that the United States could occasionally pick up minor concessions from the Soviets because they usually get very impatient to conclude sessions taking place right before holidays.

delegations have a certain sympathy for that position.) Soviet delegates are reluctant to present new ideas to their headquarters; their staffing system is cumbersome. Also, U.S. proposals provide the Soviets an opportunity to probe for weak points or fall-back positions in the U.S. approach. However, in the case of a draft treaty or formal agreement, the Soviets will try to table their own version and persuade the United States to work from it. To counter this ploy, we should either have our own draft version or quickly prepare one and use theirs to probe the Soviet position without making a commitment to negotiate therefrom.

The Soviets tend to take maximum positions with built-in redundancies, and they are not averse to changing their position 180 degrees when they consider it in their interest to do so. The U.S. negotiator, having spent weeks trying to provide a convincing rationale for his position, has great difficulty making such drastic changes.

The Soviets try to pocket the parts of the other side's proposal that they like, and ignore the rest. They use this tactic even if they have agreed in advance, as they did during SALT I, that nothing is finally agreed until everything is agreed. Moreover, they maintain an overall perspective of concurrent negotiations and sometimes attempt to play one against the other, as in MBFR versus SALT and START versus INF. They know what happens where, and are perfectly happy to transfer their positions or yours from one area into a different negotiation.[3]

As has been pointed out repeatedly, the Soviets also try to keep the scorecard even. This is particularly true in regard to compliance issues. It is also evident in recent public exchanges. They might say, "We've made five concessions; you've only made four. Why aren't you willing to keep up with us?" And they make such arguments even if our four concessions are ten times as significant as their five.

Finally, the Soviets try to capitalize on the normal U.S. desire to get the job done quickly and efficiently. In one of his early SALT I conversations with Semenov, Paul Nitze referred to the slow rate of progress. Semenov responded that Nitze should not be discouraged for in a negotiation of this type, about one-third of the business is done in the first two months, one-third during the next two years, and one-third during the last twenty minutes. The lesson here is to

---

3. Another participant suggested that the Soviet ability to coordinate across negotiations and between delegations and Moscow was often overestimated.

avoid negotiating against a deadline, because the United States usually loses. We frequently lack patience. We tend to hurry. Americans have always been noted for getting the job done quickly and efficiently. Such an approach is not always in the U.S. interest in arms control negotiations. The Soviets are masters at the waiting game and at last minute negotiation. Time is on their side. They are good poker players and excellent chess players.

SOME PROBLEMS WITH THE "LETTER OF THE LAW"

There is a set of problems in U.S.-Soviet negotiations that concerns the specificity of wording, definitions, tacit understandings, and the "spirit of the agreement"—differences regarding the "letter of the law." The Soviets usually prefer generally-worded agreements, whereas the United States prefers specificity. There are good arguments for both approaches. A choice between the two depends on the substance of the agreement or provision and what one is trying to achieve. For example, there have been arguments about what constitutes a "heavy bomber." Some say that it would be beneficial to specify precise criteria to define a heavy bomber because defense planners need such criteria to design the next generation U.S. bomber as either a medium or a heavy bomber. Others argue that if we provided such criteria, it would be too easy for the Soviets to design around them.[4] So one can argue both ways.

The Soviets like to agree first on principles and settle the details later—a "pig in the poke" approach. A related point is that accord upon definitions is extremely important, both to the understanding and the implementation of the agreement. On this matter I am perhaps biased, having been the first SCC Commissioner to try to implement the SALT I agreements (the Interim Agreement, the ABM Treaty, and the Accident Measures Agreement). The definitional problem is key. If at all possible, one should try to achieve full, formal agreement on definitions. If that is not feasible, one should endeavor to include as much mutual understanding as possible in the formal

---

4. One participant noted another problem: The United States gets entangled in so many details that we have trouble formulating our own negotiating positions, not to mention actually negotiating with the Soviets.

negotiating record. This leaves something to fall back on should a dispute arise in the future.

It is worth noting that, although we have been discussing strategic arms control since at least 1964, the United States and Soviet Union have yet to agree upon a definition of the term "strategic" in the context of strategic arms control. The Soviets use their definition, which is self-fulfilling, and we define strategic by including those systems that we want to limit. Moreover, in the 1958 Surprise Attack Conference, the two sides could not agree upon a definition of "surprise attack." Did the term refer only to an all-out missile attack? Or was it applicable to a sentry who was stabbed in the back? Finally, the ABM Treaty contains a key phrase that promises to raise controversy. Exactly what constitutes "a strategic ballistic missile or its element in flight trajectory" in the context of the ABM Treaty? "Strategic ballistic missile" is not clearly defined. One must look through the treaty negotiating record and the record at SCC negotiations over SA-5 radar testing to determine the answer to that question.

When we are negotiating an agreement, it is important to remember what is binding and what is not binding. The agreement per se and agreed statements are equally binding on both sides. But the situation differs in the cases of the SALT I Interim Agreement, the ABM Treaty, and the SALT II Treaty. In the case of SALT I, the only agreed statements that are equally binding are those initialed by Vladimir Semenov and Gerard C. Smith on the airplane to Moscow. Separate from those statements is a group of common understandings that were inserted into that agreement by Raymond Garthoff and myself by selecting from the negotiating record certain items pertinent to very controversial points. The first time the Soviets saw those common understandings was when they were submitted to Congress, because they were not discussed when the agreement was signed. Thus, the SALT I common understandings are not binding on both sides. This deficiency in SALT I was recognized in SALT II, for which the agreed statements and all the common understandings are equally binding on both sides.

Remember that there is no such thing as "spirit of the agreement" in the Soviet Union. This is an American invention that carries very little weight with the Soviets. They believe only in what is in the written agreement and in the agreed statements that they negotiate. Also, the Soviets sometimes engage in actions that are consistent with the provisions of the agreement but inconsistent with the agreement as it is presented to Congress. One should avoid, if possible, presenting to Congress interpretations of an agreement that may not be consistent with the agreement itself and the negotiating record.

These observations on Soviet negotiating practice are intended to provide additional insights for those preparing for negotiating with the U.S.S.R. or those studying Soviet negotiating style and tactics. They are not meant to be critical of U.S. negotiators but rather to highlight some differences between American and Soviet negotiating styles and approaches in a fashion that I hope will help negotiators and students.

4 OBSERVATIONS ON SOVIET NEGOTIATING PRACTICE

Howard Stoertz, Jr.

My first-hand experience in negotiating with the Soviets was in the SALT I and SALT II talks, though I have followed other U.S.–Soviet arms negotiations. Three of the four observations made in this chapter are largely based on my own experience, while the fourth is a historical note from the U.S.–Soviet alliance during World War II.

My first observation is that the basic arms control objectives that the United States and the Soviet Union currently have in common are primarily negative objectives. There is our shared fear of nuclear war and the fear that the other side will gain an advantage if we do not restrict its armament programs. Joseph Whelan, in his excellent study of Soviet negotiating behavior, noted that even antagonists can reach agreement if they have some common interest.[1] But the negative nature of the interests that we share with the Soviets calls into question the typical U.S. assumption that there is a common positive objective in arms control negotiations, which we usually call "strategic stability," and that this common objective can form a basis for mutual agreement about the kinds of weapon systems and force structures that are desirable and undesirable. Given the Soviet outlook, not only does our unilateral interpretation of "strategic stability" fall

---

1. Joseph G. Whelan, *Soviet Diplomacy and Negotiation Behavior: The Emerging New Context for U.S. Diplomacy* (Boulder, Colo.: Westview Press, 1983).

on deaf ears, but the Soviets inevitably interpret it as a way of trying to rationalize them out of their best weapon systems without paying much of a price.[2]

The Soviets approach arms control negotiations from a different perspective. In both SALT II and START, for example, they tried to slow or halt as much of our force modernization program as possible, without making a significant distinction among types of weapon systems or even types of forces. They approach negotiation from the viewpoint of a trader. "I know what I want: I want to limit U.S. force modernization as much as possible, and I want to pay the minimum possible price in terms of restrictions on my own programs." If the Soviet negotiators cannot get the limitations they want on U.S. programs at a price they are willing to pay in restrictions on their own programs, they are prepared to accept relatively modest limitations on the programs of both sides. Thus, when forced to choose, they appear to put first priority on retaining the freedom to pursue their own programs. In comparison to our approach, which assumes some sort of positive common goal, their "trading approach" to negotiations may in fact be a more realistic reflection of the relations between the two nations.

My second observation concerns the Soviet technique of trying to extract concessions. They generally offer concessions slowly and reluctantly, trying to make their opponents very grateful for even the slightest concession, and trying then to extract further concessions in exchange for every one they offer. But in my experience there is a point in the negotiations after which the Soviets tend to relax their scorekeeping style.

In 1974, after the agreement at Vladivostok providing for equal limits on U.S. and Soviet nuclear delivery vehicles, several observers jokingly remarked that the Soviets would have been well satisfied to add a short preamble and signature line to the two-page Vladivostok accord and call it a treaty. In the actual 1979 SALT II Treaty, however, there are about forty clauses that I would call limiting clauses, as well as about one hundred others that I would call implementing clauses. These latter were mostly "agreed statements," "common understandings," and so forth. They contained definitions, counting rules, aids to verification, provisions for exchange of information, etc.

2. Another participant made a similar point, asserting that the Soviets are not receptive to U.S. arguments claiming that our proposals are in their interests.

The vast majority of those hundred or so implementing clauses responded to U.S. needs.

It seems likely that after Vladivostok, at some stage, the top-level Soviet political leadership decided it was in their national interest to reach an agreement, and then instructed their delegation to "fulfill the plan." Because the United States insisted that many implementing clauses be included, the Soviet delegation found it necessary to address those issues in order to complete the agreement. In the end, the United States got most of what it wanted.

My third comment concerns our aim, in both arms control and other negotiations, gradually to erode Soviet secrecy and to bring the Soviets to a more forthcoming attitude with respect to verification needs, exchange of information, and the like. As we have proceeded with successive negotiations, we have made gains in this area, although in a very slow, piecemeal fashion. Clearly, the Soviets recognize that the satisfaction of some minimum American verification needs is one of the prices of agreement. Indeed, in recent times they have made more forthcoming offers with respect to monitoring and verification, including on-site inspections, as an inducement for us to negotiate further. Note, in particular, their offer with respect to MBFR inspectors in the fall of 1983 and their offer to permit observers for dismantling of chemical warfare stocks.

Yet considering the basic nature of Soviet society, their need for internal security and their antagonistic view toward the adversary or negotiating partner, it is questionable whether there is any near-term possibility of inducing them to accept, for example, a comprehensive or wholesale scheme for on-site inspection inside their territory. Their resistance to cooperative verification measures has eroded slowly as the arms control process has evolved, and it is reasonable to expect further progress in this area as negotiations proceed. But to expect the Soviets to accept intrusive measures that are orders of magnitude beyond anything to which they have previously agreed is simply unrealistic. The most optimistic objective one can reasonably entertain in negotiating with the Soviets is what we might call "modest agreements, frequently arrived at." It is foolish to think that we might be able to solve all of our problems, including our verification problems, with one all-encompassing deal.[3]

---

3. Several other participants commented on how verification needs might affect future U.S.-Soviet negotiations. One pointed out that negotiating adequate verification provisions

My final comment concerns the back channel issue. General John R. Deane's book, entitled *The Strange Alliance*, which he wrote on the basis of his experience as head of the U.S. military mission to Moscow in World War II, contains a very interesting lesson with respect to the use of alternate channels.[4] Deane refers to several different back channels, the principal ones being Ambassador Averell Harriman in Moscow and General George Marshall in Washington, who communicated with the highest levels of the Soviet General Staff and Defense Ministry.

There are two particularly noteworthy points to be made about Deane's experience. First, he was fully informed at all times of the communications that passed through these other channels. Second, Deane found it advantageous to initiate the use of those other channels when he needed help to resolve an impasse. These impasses arose despite the fact that we and the Soviets had at least one very positive common objective: namely, to defeat the Germans. Deane experienced great difficulty in obtaining decisions from higher command levels in the Soviet Union, as well as in implementing agreements reached in principle at higher levels. Consequently, he discovered it was beneficial to initiate personally the use of the other channels to advance the negotiations in which he was involved.

To conclude, my principal observation is that the Soviets view the U.S.-Soviet relationship as adversarial, and they enter arms negotiations as traders seeking to limit specific U.S. programs at minimum cost to their own, rather than as partners who share positive goals with us. If the United States can recognize this reality, we may be better able to avoid either euphoria or disillusionment, to accept modest but useful limitations, and to work slowly toward a safer U.S.-Soviet strategic relationship.

would get harder as military technology changes. Another added that the greater the need for on-site inspection to be able to verify an agreement, the harder it would be to negotiate that agreement. A third provided an example in the Comprehensive Test Ban, which would require a much better inspection provision than found in the Peaceful Nuclear Explosions Treaty.

4. John R. Deane, *The Strange Alliance: The Story of Our Efforts at Wartime Cooperation with Russia* (New York; Viking Press, 1946).

5 TEN COMMANDMENTS FOR NEGOTIATING WITH THE SOVIET UNION

Edward L. Rowny

This chapter presents a list of ten commandments, which are general lessons learned from reflections on my negotiating experience. It is not difficult to find exceptions to these rules; I could offer exceptions myself. However, the rules are valid more often than not.

Before joining the SALT II negotiations, I read the accounts of several negotiators, including Dean Acheson, Dean Rusk, George Kennan, and others, who had negotiated with both Soviets (post-revolution) and Russians (pre-revolution). Based on this research, I compiled a list of ten commandments and checked them with about ten experienced negotiators. Then I tacked those commandments on my desk in Geneva. The U.S. negotiating team subsequently violated nine of the ten. We did try not to violate them, but such violations are in the nature of things. It is hard not to transgress those commandments.

I subsequently drew up a revised list of the ten commandments, drawn from my own negotiating experience. I looked back only to early 1973, when I joined Ambassador U. Alexis Johnson's negotiating team. These revised commandments are discussed below.

As a caveat, let me say that I do not claim to be omniscient. I am sure you will be glad to learn that. I am a product of my own experience; my views are admittedly somewhat subjective. And since there is nothing new under the sun, experienced negotiators already know my commandments. Finally, be aware that each of these commandments has contradictions and exceptions.

THE TEN COMMANDMENTS

1. Thou shalt remember above all thy objective.[1] The Soviets have better defined, more clear-cut, longer-range objectives than we do. Many Americans find the nature of those objectives debatable. Regardless, we are problem solvers, inheriters of the Greek rationalist tradition who believe that all problems have solutions if only we try hard enough. The Soviets view negotiations differently. They are more competitive. They do not believe that all problems have solutions. Also, whereas we think in terms of four-year presidential election cycles, they think in terms of longer time periods, decades longer.

In the past, we have made arms control the centerpiece of our foreign policy. That is a mistake the Reagan administration has tried to avoid. Arms control is an important element of foreign policy, but it should not be the central focus. The Soviets are better at putting the military at the cutting edge of their foreign policy.

As a general rule, the Soviets first set their objectives and then shape their forces to realize those objectives. They allow arms control to restructure their forces only insofar as this fits the objectives. In contrast, the United States has tended to reverse that pyramid. Too often we have placed arms control at the center of our foreign policy, and we have reshaped our military forces to satisfy the dictates of arms control. As a result, we do not know how to utilize most effectively the forces that we have. Perhaps this is an exaggeration, but the basic point is valid.

2. Thou shalt be patient. Insofar as the Soviets place arms control in a larger context, they are prepared to wait for a shift in the correlation

---

1. There was considerable discussion on the subject of objectives. One participant suggested that the fact that our proposals are normally compromises among competing bureaucratic interests makes them hard to negotiate. Numerous participants voiced the view that general negotiating objectives must be understood and accepted by the public. Some also argued that the formulation of our objectives should account for possible common U.S.-Soviet interests, such as the prevention of nuclear war. One went further, asserting that the existence of shared objectives is not enough to set the stage for a successful negotiation. We also need, he said, agreement on the role of arms control in serving those common interests. Finally, someone stated that we also need to prioritize among negotiating objectives to ensure that we achieve our most important ones.

of forces that serves their political ends. Although arms control is not a game, it is enlightening to note the different games we and they play in our spare time. The Soviets play chess; we play Pac Man. They like the well-thought-through results of step-by-step reasoning. We like the instant results of electronic machines.

The late Soviet Premier Nikita Khrushchev once said that Foreign Minister Andrei Gromyko was very patient. "I tell him to sit on a cake of ice," he said, "and he'll sit there." That is true. Someone else has quipped that Gromyko not only sits there, he does not melt the ice. It has also been said that the term "sangfroid" was invented to describe Gromyko. In contrast, we are quite impatient, and our desire for instant results hurts us.

3. Thou shalt keep secrets. By tradition, history, and type of government, Soviet society is closed, secretive. The Soviets, of course, are not constrained by public opinion to the extent that we are. They play their cards close to the chest, while we play ours face-up on the table. They can obtain our secrets from the media, but it is more difficult for us to discover their secrets. This makes verification very difficult and to some extent one-sided. The Soviets have suggested that we should dispense with verification. "Let us trust one another," they say. They want our trust but refuse to provide us the access to information that is the basis of trust. Such trust is a one-way street. They do not have to rely on trust because we cannot keep secrets.

4. Thou shalt bear in mind the differences in political structures. It is obvious, but worth restating, that our political structure is completely and profoundly different from theirs. They have a centralized authority with nothing comparable to our truly independent legislature or a ratification process. Their society imposes laws from the top, whereas our leaders derive their powers from the consent of the governed. De Tocqueville made this point 140 years ago, but it cannot be repeated often enough.

5. Thou shalt beware of Greeks bearing gifts. This refers to the question of compromise. The Soviets view compromise differently than we do. They acknowledge the necessity of trade-offs, but they are very macho about it. The word *kompromis* is not a native Russian word, but a word acquired from other languages. Also, the Soviet economic system is centralized, whereas ours is mercantilist. And their social system provides few lessons in the art of compromise. Thus, it is not surprising that they view compromise as a weakness, and that they find it difficult to make compromises.

Future negotiators should remember that the Soviets will pocket anything they are given. Although they say that nothing is agreed until everything is agreed, they try to claim all of our tentative concessions as final. So one must be careful not to make too many conciliatory gestures. I learned this early in my negotiating career. Discussing a particular problem over drinks with one of the Soviet generals, I told him the problem was easy. It could be divided into six parts. We could give them A, B, and C if they could give us D, E, and F. The following day I presented this idea as a formal proposal. After I offered them A, B, and C, they walked out. I protested that I had not finished. They insisted I had finished; I had told them what we were prepared to concede, and they had accepted. At the next week's meeting, I suggested that if they could give us D, E, and F, we would offer reciprocal concessions. They responded that they were not idiots and that they do not negotiate that way.

Another example harks back to a U.S.-Soviet boat ride on Lake Geneva. I began playing my harmonica in an effort to encourage friendlier interactions with the Soviets. Our secretaries danced with the Soviets, and everyone had a good time. At the end of the festivities, the head of the Soviet SALT I delegation, Vladimir Semenov, took up a collection of rubles, dollars, and French and Swiss francs. He grinned and said, "O.K., we will split it 50–50." Then, he put all the money in his pocket. "What do you mean 50–50?," I asked. And he replied, "Well, you had 50 percent of the pleasure by playing. I get 50 percent of the pleasure by spending the money." That is how the Soviets operate. They follow the maxim that what is mine is mine, and what is yours is negotiable. This is an extreme example, but not altogether out of character.

6. Thou shalt remember that in the Soviet view, form is substance. The head of·their START delegation, Victor Karpov, expressed that view in those exact words. The Soviets believe that the number of people at the negotiating table, the size of the table, and the agenda are all important issues. In the past, the United States tended to concede on such matters. Thus, Karpov protested when I refused to concede on certain "formalities." "Why are you being so hard-nosed?," he questioned. "You are simply blocking progress." I suggested that he could meet me half-way for the sake of progress, but he refused.

To give another example, at the beginning of START, we had agreed that each side should have "one and five" (one negotiator and five delegates). Then, the Soviets arrived at a meeting with "one and six." I protested that we had agreed to one and five. He said that it did not matter. I said it did matter; two of his delegates would be pitted against one of mine. So we recessed while I summoned one of my senior advisers and made him a delegate. Thus, when we reconvened, we each had one and six. Karpov understood my message, and the negotiation continued. The moral of the story is that we must let the Soviets know that we know that form can influence substance.

7. Thou shalt not be deceived by the Soviet "fear of being invaded." Granted, the Soviets have been invaded by the Tartars, the Poles, the Swedes, the French, and the Germans. But they themselves have invaded the Crimea, Finland, Siberia, Latvia, Lithuania, Estonia, Hungary, Czechoslovakia, and Afghanistan, to name a few. The record is mixed. On the one hand, they do have a defensive attitude and do remember being invaded. On the other hand, they did not come to occupy one-sixth of the world's space simply by being invaded.

Thus, to some extent, the Soviet government invokes an external threat to establish its domestic legitimacy. From an early age, Soviet children are taught about the Russian history of being invaded. This breeds a fear of invasion and a strong preoccupation with national defense. These feelings are associated with the Russians strong emotional attachment to Mother Russia. Even the dissidents long for Mother Russia. However, we understand too little about the true psychology of the Soviet people and perhaps less about their leadership.

The Soviets themselves tell us that equality is not their guiding principle but that they insist on equality *plus* "equal security." However, they believe that to be equal, they must be more equal. In other words, equal sequrity really means Soviet superiority. For this reason we cannot accept their demands that equal security be added to equality.

8. Thou shalt beware of negotiating in the eleventh hour. The Soviets are masters of eleventh-hour negotiations. Granted, they made numerous concessions in those last weeks of the SALT II talks before June 17. (June 14 and 15 were especially active days.) But we thought we had an agreement at 4:00 PM on the 15th—until they raised a few more issues. We then had two more sessions at 8:00 PM and 10:00 PM. Finally, at one minute to midnight, they agreed on the final points. We had been waiting patiently for the last twenty minutes of the negotiating round, and our patience had paid off. We should operate this way more often.[2]

9. Thou shalt not be deceived by the Soviets' words. Under Secretary of Defense Fred Ikle has done an excellent study on what he calls "semantic infiltration." Years of dialogue with the Soviets have taught me that words mean what they want them to mean. They call East Germany the "German Democratic Republic," although it is neither democratic nor a republic. They call their troops in Afghanistan "freedom fighters;" the opposition they term "rebels." They use words to try to mesmerize us and put us at a disadvantage.

10. Thou shalt not misinterpret the human element. Karpov and I had a businesslike arrangement. He was very ornery in SALT II, but he mellowed somewhat in START. Sometimes, after publicly criticizing the United States, he would privately say to me, "Don't take that seriously. I had to say that for the record." This politeness in private is fine. But keep in mind that it is worth little to strike an agreement over vodka in the evening, because it will be publicly repudiated the next day. The Soviets can be pleasant, but they are dedicated communists. In sum, there is no such thing as a truly friendly Soviet. At least, I have not met one in my ten years of negotiating.

The Soviets, in general, are on a short leash, but they are very worthy opponents. They do their homework and are dedicated. Also, they are pragmatic enough to reverse their position on an issue when it is in their interest to do so.

This leads us to the problem of how much to pad our opening proposal in a negotiation. I do not think it is possible to adhere rigidly to one's opening position, no matter how "reasonable" it is. In the first place, the Soviets do not understand that approach. They insist on trading one concession for another. In the second place, Americans generally view negotiations as a matter of give and take. Even if our opening position is quite conciliatory, the American public will expect us to make further concessions to secure an agreement. Thus,

---

2. Several participants commented on deadlines. One said that progress in a negotiation was only possible if political events were used to drive a negotiation along. Thus, we must be prepared to negotiate in the eleventh hour. Another agreed that we should accept the inevitability of deadlines and think about how we can use them to our advantage. A third added that deadlines are a problem for us only if they are one-sided. He argued that if both face them, they can facilitate agreement.

to satisfy both the Soviets and our own people, it is necessary to build some negotiating room into any opening position. [3]

The issue of the Soviet attitude toward morality is a controversial one. I believe that they would rather lie or cheat than be accused of stupidity. The Soviets view negotiation as a competition and will take advantage of any loopholes that we are shortsighted enough to allow them. They do not consider this sort of behavior to be lying or cheating. Their approach to morality is different from ours. Whatever they do as a service to their country they consider to be morally irreproachable. Granted, they will generally abide by the letter of an agreement once it is written in fine print. The trick is getting them to sign the fine print. This is particularly difficult because conscientious attention to detail often elicits charges from them that we are stalling the negotiation.

It is important not to embarrass or humiliate one's adversary in negotiations. The opponent must always be given a graceful way out. This is a problem in the negotiations on INF. The Soviets painted themselves into a box. However, they can get out of it. It would be unwise for us to propose a way out because they would simply negotiate on that offer. The proper approach is to let them know that we understand their problem and that we are going to be patient. Moreover, we must let them know that we are willing to consider any proposal they advance.

CONCLUSION

In sum, the above ten commandments are intended to be practical tools for negotiators. They help explain why the Soviets' job is some-

---

3. The matter of the opening position was identified as one of the most crucial in a negotiation. Several participants voiced support for opening negotiations with a position reasonably close to what we want, which avoids the problem of establishing a record of making concessions, both a domestic political and a negotiating problem. However, some participants did express concern about U.S. positions that appear too inflexible.

Alternative approaches to the opening position dilemma were also suggested. One idea was to use the opening rounds of a negotiation to sound out the Soviets and perhaps come to some agreement with them on principles before committing to an opening position. One person mentioned that these sorts of exploratory talks had met with some success in the past. Another idea drew from the approach taken in the U.S. position at the INF talks, where we defined a set of criteria that an agreement must meet and said we would consider any offer that met those criteria. Finally, it was suggested that we could offer several alternative proposals instead of only one, thereby avoiding the problem of seeming to "lose" when we make a concession.

what easier than ours. The commandments rarely offer solutions; rather, they define questions and hint at some answers.

Our current lack of knowledge highlights the need to study the Soviets more thoroughly. It is particularly important to learn the language. I insisted that every member of my delegation learn Russian, and five out of six now know it to some extent. It is not necessary to be fluent, but it is good to know enough so that when the Soviets whisper amongst themselves, we can say, *"Eto ne tak"* ("It's not like that"). This keeps them on their toes. Learning the language also opens up more avenues for understanding the Soviets. We would do well to learn about their history, their culture, their motivations.

6 LESSONS LEARNED IN BILATERAL NEGOTIATIONS

Paul C. Warnke

My experience in negotiations with the Soviet Union was relatively brief — less than two years. However, I do have a number of impressions that I would like to pass on. The first set has to do with the nature of the negotiations themselves. One of the real problems in arms control is that neither side needs a deal. It is not like a labor negotiation, where eventually there has to be some sort of settlement or the factory shuts down and the people are out of work. In the arms control field, agreement is voluntary. Moreover, in many instances, the negotiations proceed for reasons other than trying to achieve an agreement.

The MBFR talks are an example of a round of negotiations conceived in sin: Neither side really needs a deal. We entered into MBFR in 1973 to fend off the Mansfield Resolution, that is, to eliminate some of the pressures for unilateral withdrawal of American forces in Europe. For the Soviets, MBFR is part of the price that they paid for discussions on mutual security and for ratification of the post–World War II boundaries. The fact that neither side needs a deal contributes to the extraordinary difficulty negotiators face in trying to reach agreement. There are other difficult factors, of course. For example, Europe is a geographic area in which reductions on the Western side are genuine reductions, as compared with nothing but redeployment for the East. Regardless, MBFR illustrates the problems associated with a negotiation that is undertaken for reasons other than trying to get a deal.[1]

A second observation is that the result of an arms control negotiation must be good for both sides, or it is good for nothing at all. It is not like a commercial negotiation where one can out-trade the other side and then insist on the benefits of one's deal. This is because an arms control agreement is not subject to enforcement by any central authority. The instance in which Nicaragua tried unsuccessfully to make the United States accept the jurisdiction of the International Court of Justice demonstrates the consensual nature of its process. So even if there were not an escape clause in an arms control agreement, if either side were to conclude that it had been outtraded, it would repudiate the agreement as being inconsistent with that side's supreme interests. Thus, we must acknowledge the unfortunate fact that, contrary to the American spirit of winning, the best one can hope for is a draw—a draw that is good for both sides. Neither side will sign an agreement that leaves it worse off than it was before.[2]

This is one reason why the American public is impatient with the arms control process. They always want to know who won. So the negotiators are under pressure to open with a position that straddles that fine edge between being totally ludicrous and being marginally responsive. Moreover, it is politically difficult to alter that initial position.

In March 1977 the Carter administration opened its SALT II negotiations with a proposal that straddled that fine line. It was not quite silly, but at the same time it was not a proposal that the Soviet Union would accept. The best we could hope was that the Soviet Union would devise a counterproposal that would provide a basis for negotiations. But politically, we found ourselves saddled with the opening position, and any further change in that position was regarded as a retreat, as a concession, as an admission we were not really tough

1. A participant pointed out that there may occasionally be an American domestic political need for an agreement, which the Soviets may be able to exploit in negotiations.

2. In the same vein, one participant argued that both sides need to demonstrate more willingness to discuss areas in which they have an advantage. Another argued that we have had so little success in arms control because we usually advanced proposals that are designed to improve our security and blunt Soviet strategy. He suggested that instead each side should openly state what it wants and try to reach common ground given these desires.

negotiators.[3] Perhaps one way to avoid that is to be less public about one's bargaining positions. To hold a press conference on one side's view of the merits simply sparks a press conference on the other side. As a result, both sides become less responsive than they might be if the negotiations were less publicized.

My third set of comments is on the characteristics of Soviet negotiations. When I became head of the SALT delegation, the negotiations had been underway for more than seven years. Consequently, many ground rules were fairly well established. The interpreters had worked out an extraordinarily effective liaison. Many of the early problems experienced by Ambassador Gerard Smith, our chief SALT I negotiator, were behind us. It had become formalized, like a classical ballet.

It seems to me that there is no way to avoid the plenary sessions, in which both sides read their positions to one another. In these plenaries, after I finished my prepared statement, Minister Vladimir Semenov, the chief Soviet negotiator, always said that he would give it the attention it deserved. At least, that is the way it came out in the translation. Naturally, this cast a slight chill on the proceedings!

The negotiations also included what we laughingly referred to as the "informal sessions." In dealing with Minister Semenov, these were anything but informal. He would have a prepared brief on any issue that he anticipated might be raised. I would raise the issue, he would reach for his brief, and the only moments of spontaneity would be when the interpreter picked up the wrong translation. If I raised an issue on which he had not been briefed, he would adjourn the meeting. Semenov simply was not a man to engage in any sort of ad hoc discussions. At one plenary session, I made the tactical error of responding extemporaneously to his formal presentation. Later, Victor Karpov, who was Ambassador Rowny's sparring mate in the START talks, approached my deputy, Ralph Earle, requesting that Ambassador Warnke not speak extemporaneously. Karpov said that it made

3. This comment sparked a discussion of the lessons of the March 1977 experience. Some participants said the subsequent history of SALT shows we should have stuck with this far-reaching proposal (which required deep cuts in Soviet forces) because the Soviets would eventually have accepted it. Others argued that it was too radical a departure from the then-existing SALT regime. In appearing to jettison this regime, they said, the United States made it hard for the Soviets to accept it. Still others pointed out that this same problem existed with the more recent U.S. proposals in START.

the Minister nervous; he did not like anything that departed from the set format.

This rigidity is not necessarily characteristic of the Soviet style of negotiations. Just before the first session of the Indian Ocean talks, for instance, Soviet chief negotiator Ambassador Lev Mendelevich asked me to meet with him at the Soviet Mission in Berne. His opening comment was that I would find him very different from Minister Semenov. He said he was not Russian, he was Lithuanian, and he was Jewish. Indeed, as he promised, his negotiating style was very different from Semenov's. He liked to extemporize. In fact, he sometimes extended meetings far beyond the appointed time limit simply because he enjoyed the exchange. This did not necessarily allow for greater progress, but the meetings were certainly less structured.

Ambassador Mendelevich was not the only Soviet negotiator who liked to extemporize. This was also characteristic of Chairman Petrosyants who, oddly enough, made almost the same comment to me as did Mendelevich—that I would find him different from Igor Morokov, his predecessor as head of the comprehensive test ban (CTB) negotiations. "You see, I am not Russian. I am Armenian," he explained. Indeed, he was a much more ebullient person.

Of course, it is not difficult to be more ebullient than Semenov. It was very hard to explore possible changes with Minister Semenov. He would not play what I have referred to as the "what if" game. I might say to him, "Although we don't have the authority to depart from our established positions, if I were able to get my principals to make this sort of change, what do you think you could do?" Semenov would never take that gambit.

In part, this was a product of his background and experience. I was once told of an incident when Semenov, then stationed in East Germany, was called back to Russia. At the time, he was on a weekend inspection trip, so his deputy seized the opportunity to return to Moscow and hobnob with the top men. The deputy was ushered into the presence of Lavrenti Beria, then the head of the secret police, and shot. Whether this particular story is true or not, it would not be too atypical of the experiences of people in Semenov's generation who grew up under Stalin's regime. That episode may well explain Semenov's unwillingness to exceed his instructions or even to explore possible alternatives.

Thus, while Semenov headed the Soviet delegation, changes in the Soviet position usually had to be negotiated outside of Geneva. This could frequently be done with Ambassador Anatoliy Dobrynin, who had played that back channel role during the SALT I negotiations. Dobrynin provided a means of "thinking out loud," without any commitments, in an effort to break a particular logjam. Even so, it was usually very hard to make progress.

It is difficult to suggest ways in which the negotiating process might be improved because so much depends on personnel, on relationships, on the particular impulses of an administration at a given time. Nevertheless, if the president of the United States wants an arms control agreement, he can structure the process to get an agreement. It requires close coordination between Washington and the negotiating front. It requires a secretary of state who is thoroughly versed in the problems and who is able to participate on a regular basis. We would never have been able to solve the major problems of SALT II had the discussions been restricted to the negotiating teams because the teams had a limited ability to speculate and to explore possible changes in each other's positions. Although high-level contacts were often time-consuming, without them the positions would have remained fairly rigid.

The classic example of this point is the Vladivostok meeting in 1974. The SALT II negotiations could not have been completed if President Ford and Soviet Party Chairman Leonid Brezhnev had not met face-to-face and resolved the central problem that was effectively preventing completion of the treaty. This was the principle of equal ceilings. Before Vladivostok, the Soviets insisted (as they have been doing in the negotiations on INF) that they were entitled to compensation for the nuclear powers they face other than the United States. They wanted something like a continuation of the numerical discrepancy that existed in the SALT I Interim Agreement. We knew that an agreement that provided the Soviet forces with an advantage would not have been politically feasible. Also, the Jackson Amendment, passed during consideration of the SALT I Treaty and Agreement, stated explicitly that any future treaty must include the principle of equality. It was during the Vladivostok meeting that Brezhnev finally recognized that an "equal ceilings" provision was a necessary precondition for an agreement.

The difference between the U.S. and Soviet decisionmaking processes has a significant effect on negotiations. Within the Soviet Union there is nothing comparable to our interagency working groups. There is no backstopping group on an interagency basis that can handle problems that are unearthed during negotiations and develop positions that are responsive to those problems. Instead, when a position has to be changed within the Soviet decisionmaking apparatus, the change evolves through the separate agencies such as the Foreign Ministry or the Defense Ministry. Then, everything has to be resolved at the top. It is as though the National Security Council had to convene whenever a minor change is proposed in a U.S. negotiating position.[4]

In some respects, this gives the Soviets an advantage because it does conduce to rigidity. It makes them stick with a position, unwilling to change it because it is so difficult to change. This means that U.S. negotiators must periodically drive the Soviet negotiators back to Moscow. We have to make it clear that there is an impasse, and that as a consequence a change must be made.

For example, in the CTB talks, we considered several issues absolutely essential. For one, we refused to make exceptions for peaceful nuclear explosions (PNEs). The then head of the Soviet delegation, Igor Morokov, was also the man in charge of PNEs within the Soviet government. Thus, he had a vested institutional interest in making allowances for PNEs. Repeatedly he showed me movies demonstrating the great things that could be accomplished by underground explosions, such as diverting streams and breaking up mineral beds. For obvious reasons, we rejected the idea of an exception for peaceful nuclear explosions. We also felt that on-site inspection was necessary in a comprehensive test ban. And we insisted that the Soviets permit the stationing of American seismic stations on Soviet territory. All three issues initially were resisted with no give whatsoever.

Eventually, in the latter part of 1977, Morokov went to Moscow. Upon his return, he conceded to us on all three points. He could not have done this himself, nor could it have been done gradually. This is a consequence of the Soviet decisionmaking system. They are very

4. There was considerable discussion about the Soviet decisionmaking process, particularly regarding the relative roles of the Foreign Ministry and military officials. One participant said the military set the limits on what could be conceded in talks and the diplomats maneuvered within those limits. Another pointed out that the Foreign Ministry gained clout in this area when former Foreign Minister Andrei Gromyko grew increasingly powerful. A third participant said that on substantive matters the respective roles had reversed. In SALT, the military was more hard-line and polemical; in START, the diplomats assumed this role. Finally, a participant observed that we are handicapped in negotiations because we are primarily dealing with government officials, whereas it is the party that makes all the decisions.

poor at compromising. As a result, they sometimes collapse totally and give the other side its maximum position.[5]

This happened, for example, in the controversy over cruise missile range. We argued at length in the SALT talks about how to measure the range of a cruise missile. We maintained that it should not be measured in a straight line because a cruise missile does not fly like a crow; it has to check off certain landmarks to find its way to its goal. Moreover, as the talks progressed, we argued that we had to provide maneuvering room to enable our cruise missiles to take evasive tactics. So, eventually we were requesting roughly a 35 percent increase over the straight line distance. The Soviets simply could not deal with that particular problem. After a meeting between Soviet Foreign Minister Andrei Gromyko and Secretary Cyrus Vance, Gromyko presented us two alternatives: Either the range would be measured in a straight line, or there would be no limit. We chose to set no limit, a much better outcome from our point of view. We were prepared to accept a compromise, but the Soviet system could not handle that particular issue in a fashion that permitted compromise.

In view of the differences between our decisionmaking systems, we have to expect a degree of Soviet rigidity. They maintain a particular position for as long as possible. However, we can elicit concessions by making it clear that we cannot accept their position and that therefore it has to change. This will usually drive them back to Moscow and ideally result in a high-level discussion that will enable agreement to be reached and progress to continue.

5. Two participants expressed agreement with this idea that the Soviets sometimes make sweeping concessions after holding rigidly to a position for a long time. Another disagreed with the characterization that they "collapsed" in negotiation, suggesting that they took basically a "scorekeeping" approach to concessions and tried to make sure that they were at least even.

7 NEGOTIATING WITH THE SOVIETS: GETTING PAST NO

Walter Slocombe

I have chosen the title of this chapter with due apologies to Roger Fisher. One fact that we have to acknowledge about the Soviet Union is that the Russians are different, and that consequently our relationship with them is very different from our relationship with most other countries in the world. But it is an open question whether *negotiating* with the Soviet Union, if context could be held constant, is all that different as a process from negotiating with any other nation. There are certainly some important and relevant cultural differences. But most of the problems of negotiating with the Soviets arise because our dealings with them are in a very different context from what we usually call "negotiations." We must try to understand how negotiations in ordinary life—personal, commercial, even international— differ from the situations in which we face the Soviets, and also how they are sometimes the same.

CONTEXTS FOR NEGOTIATION

First, there is, to some degree in life generally, but certainly in international affairs and especially with Soviets, what might be called a "myth of negotiability"—the notion that almost everything can be solved if people would only sit down and talk about it. It is certainly almost always useful, given the alternatives, to make sure one has tried to negotiate a problem with an adversary. But the theory that most problems can be solved by talking about them is a theory of psychotherapy, not a theory of international relations. Some problems simply cannot be solved by any amount of talk. In a recent article, Ambassador Paul Nitze cites a comment by a former British diplomat that negotiating with the Soviets is like dealing with a defective vending machine. If you put a coin in and nothing comes out, there are various things you can do, but one thing is sure: There is no point in just talking to it.[1]

The context issue of greatest importance here is asking why negotiation can lead to agreement. A first class of "negotiable" contexts is that in which people negotiate to agreement because they know that if they do not agree between themselves, somebody else will decide for them. And they feel that they can negotiate a better solution for themselves than an external party. Settlements on almost all litigation and in other situations where issues would otherwise be referred to higher authority, whether the government's decisional bodies or other kinds of authorities, are produced by this impetus. Obviously, this context for successful negotiation has very little relevance to international affairs in general, but it is at the core of a great deal of negotiations that go on in the world.

A second reason why people negotiate successfully, which does have some application internationally, is that they want to sustain a useful common relationship despite a current dispute over some part of the relationship. This is true of all family disputes and of a great many commercial and business deals. In general, a business deal is never struck up unless people want an agreement—and it usually does not survive their ceasing to want it. If one side wants to buy and the other does not want to sell, then the buyer finds somebody else who does want to sell and works out a deal. Many labor agreements and almost all disputes at a direct plant level or office level fall into this category.

I participated in the effort to write the 1984 Democratic Party platform, the classic example of a situation where people are prepared to compromise many differences, adjust on a lot of issues, make many verbal concessions, and perhaps even make some real concessions.

1. Paul H. Nitze, "Living with the Soviets," *Foreign Affairs,* Vol. 63, no. 2 (Winter 1984–85): 360–74.

These people are willing to negotiate for their common, broader interest — not necessarily the party's winning, but their not being perceived as the people who made trouble or who could not keep other people from making trouble.

The fact of some negotiations succeeding because of a mutual desire to keep a relationship going is not unknown, of course, in international relations. It is certainly responsible for allowing the United States to reach agreements with allied countries and other countries with whom we have generally friendly relations. Sometimes to get international problems solved by negotiation, it is necessary to broaden the focus and involve people who perceive an interest in the overall relationship, not just in the immediate dispute. For example, a few years ago there was a big dispute about the import of American citrus fruit into France, about which the Department of Agriculture was in a rage. One goal of the negotiations in this case was to expand the range of people who were aware of this dispute over $40 million worth of citrus fruit and to suggest that the United States might have some other interests with the French that would make it inadvisable to sell out to Sunkist on the question.

The success stories about U.S.-Soviet negotiations often arise in this context, where we have an agreed common interest and so are able to work out a deal. But the range of our common interests with the Soviet Union is extraordinarily narrow — and that poses a real problem for U.S.-Soviet negotiations. We have only a very limited number of important contacts of any kind. Witness the problems we experienced in drawing up a list of possible sanctions to impose against the Soviet Union for its actions in Poland or Afghanistan. The list of links between us is so short and so petty compared to what is at stake. We can cut off cultural exchanges, we can embargo ballerinas. If we choose to be more forceful, we can stop selling grain. But cutting off grain sales is by far the most serious sanction we can impose, and it obviously does no fundamental damage to Soviet interests. Indeed, in light of the relatively autarkic nature of the Soviet economy, no economic links are likely to be critical, either in terms of improving them as an inducement to agreement or reducing them as pressure.

One of the major sources of the ostensible historical "negotiating lessons" about dealing with the Russians is the World War II period, when we were genuinely confused about the nature of our relationship with the Soviet Union. We believed then that relationship was, and certainly ought to be, like our relationship with Britain. We believed we were common partners against Hitler and had a vast number of common interests. We thought it self-evident that anything that advanced the cause of the coalition should be warmly welcomed. So we believed U.S. and Soviet officials ought to be willing to make sacrifices for the common cause, or at least ought not be totally self-interested. Clearly the Soviets never saw it that way.

Our expectations in this regard were repeatedly disappointed: The effort to arrange for American bombers to land in Soviet-controlled territory, the effort to get the Soviets to move at the time of the uprising in Warsaw, and a lot of the negotiations during and after the war intended to plan for the immediate post-war period were frustrated. Throughout the historical accounts of these attempts there is a sense of profound disillusionment. What we learned were not really lessons on negotiating, but lessons about the *real* relationship between the United States and the Soviet Union during the war and since. We approached the negotiations in the belief that the United States and the Soviet Union had a broad commonality of interests that should help particular conflicts; they didn't. That difference in judgments about the relationship—not different negotiating styles—produced great frustration and endless failure to agree.

A third major reason why adversaries who lack these other two reasons for negotiating may do so is because they wish to avoid the risks of an all-out confrontation. This is a major impetus for much compromising in labor–management disputes where the costs of a prolonged strike appear too high for those who would have to pay. And it is clearly the main reason that the United States and the Soviet Union negotiate.[2]

In this regard, we need further study of U.S.–Soviet negotiating during what were probably the two most intense crises of our time— the Cuban missile crisis and the 1973 Arab–Israeli War. On those two occasions, both sides realized that if they did not work out a compromise, they would face more immediately than ever before the risk of a war, or at least a much higher level of confrontation than they wanted to face. I have not studied the record carefully, but I have a sense that the so-called "laws" of Soviet negotiating behavior would not apply well to the way the U.S.–Soviet negotiations were actually conducted during these crises.

---

2. A commentator suggested that negotiations could be used not only to avoid conflict, but also to limit it if it occurs by establishing rules for its pursuit.

Of course, most people who believe in arms control, and I certainly count myself as one of them,[3] believe that the Soviets are interested in arms control as a means of avoiding all-out confrontation. Not only is there the common interest in physical survival and avoiding nuclear war, but also a more subtle and complicated sense of why they do not want to press the competition to the limit, even short of war. The Soviets are afraid of American technology, and the Americans are somewhat afraid of Soviet technology and also of the Soviet ability to pour their resources into solving a military problem. Thus, neither side wants to drive the other to an ultimate test of comparative advantage, much less the ultimate test of a nuclear war. It is under circumstances where the primary impetus for successful U.S.–Soviet negotiations—to avoid the consequences of confrontation—operates that arms control negotiations work, if they work at all.[4]

There is a fourth reason why adversaries negotiate, which is very important to why the United States and the Soviet Union engage with each other in such a process. That is the desire to be perceived as negotiating—not necessarily the desire to reach an agreement. Although this is generally not the case with other countries, it is quite common between the United States and the Soviet Union. For both sides, negotiations have been a form of public relations, a form of propaganda, a form of theater. This seems to be true of the MBFR negotiations, or at least how they have been used by both sides.[5] It is unclear whether these talks are intended to produce results or are intended to produce further negotiations.

PERCEPTIONS AND MISPERCEPTIONS ABOUT NEGOTIATING WITH THE SOVIETS

Perhaps the basic lesson of negotiating with the Soviets is that there is only a limited range of contexts—a crucial, but limited range—

3. Mr. Slocombe added in discussion that, in his view, arms control has been a substantial technical success because its effect has been to make us safer, though prudence requires demonstrating that we can ensure our security without arms control, if necessary.

4. Other participants agreed that the concern about all-out confrontation was a fundamental impetus for U.S.–Soviet arms control efforts, though some warned against overemphasizing this U.S.–Soviet commonality (see Chapter 2, p. 27).

5. See Chapter 9 for a lengthy discussion of MBFR.

where there is much reason to expect success. As for the more specific lessons about techniques and tactics, they are not unique to U.S.-Soviet negotiations. Many are commonplace in any negotiation. For example, it is very important to be clear about objectives—to know what the other side wants and have a good idea about what your side wants.[6] The INF negotiations in particular are a brilliant example of the United States adopting certain basic principles that, we have made clear throughout, will not change. The parameters of the U.S. INF position could be summarized as a bilateral U.S.-Soviet agreement that provides equal levels and is global in scope. Within those parameters, the United States is prepared to do a lot of different things a lot of different ways if that helps, but it is not prepared to compromise its basic principles.[7] This clarity about basic principles helps immensely in formulating our position, responding to Soviet proposals, and sustaining allied support.

Another example is the MBFR negotiations, in which the United States and its allies have rightly established a basic position from which we have been unwilling to budge. (The fact that this has led to an impasse in the negotiations does not make it a mistake.) That position is that the MBFR agreements are intended to preserve security and are not to be based on fake data. A clear position such as this is not necessarily a harbinger of progress, but it does allow a negotiator to be more clear about what he does and does not want.

It is also imperative in any negotiations to have a sense of priority. The effort to preserve everything or to attain everything with no sense of priority, has never been successful in negotiations. When everything is vital, nothing is vital. One may or may not agree with the priorities that were adopted, for example, in the SALT II negotiations, so far as preserving U.S. options was concerned. But there *were* some, and they were successfully carried out. First, the agreement was not to limit air-launched cruise missiles in any way or seriously inhibit the way in which the United States planned to deploy those missiles. Second, the agreement was to allow the MX program to go forward. These may seem the wrong priorities to some, but they were clearly important technical priorities, and they were preserved

6. See Chapter 5, p. 48 for further discussion of objectives.

7. Another participant described the INF approach as a firm commitment to general criteria and a willingness to consider offers that satisfy them. He agreed that this approach could serve as a useful model for future negotiations.

throughout. In some other situations, where we have been even less clear about our priorities, we have been even less successful in achieving them.

In addition to those basic principles of negotiating with anyone, there are some particular cultural differences that influence U.S.-Soviet negotiations. The Soviets have something of a counting mentality about concessions that elicits some highly predictable behavior about major meetings on arms control. There is always *a* Soviet concession. It may not be very big or very important, but it is always *a* concession and a genuine concession. It is a change from a previous position in a direction that we have at least indicated we wanted them to go. We occasionally change our minds and wish they had not done it, but they have made *a* concession. This opens up room for one of their favorite arguments: "Well, we've made a concession, why don't you make a concession? Preferably *two*, considering the huge scope and importance of our concession."

Much has been written and many practitioners have ideas about the human side of negotiation with the Soviets. It was my consistent observation, at the high-level meetings that I attended, that the first meeting is invariably unpleasant. There are two theories about why this is so. One is that the Soviets make an effort to intimidate the Americans, attempting to bully them into some concession they would not otherwise make. I was always more attracted to the second argument, which suggests that they are thinking something like: "Well, we will try one more time, and if the ice breaks by surprise, then we won't have given up unnecessarily." That pattern is probably more typical of the Soviets.

It is sometimes said that the Soviets do not like technical complexity. They certainly do not see much use for it when we propose complete and detailed agreements mostly for reasons of verification. They are, however, perfectly prepared to accept bafflingly complicated technical points if we insist on them and make it clear that they are important. The "new types" definition in SALT II and the radar rules in the ABM Treaty are clear examples of that.

One peculiarity of Soviet negotiations is that the Soviets appear to regard it as a favor to explain their own position. For example, the Soviets said, in the START talks, that there should be a limit on the number of "charges." For months and months it remained unclear what they intended that limit might be or even what they meant by "charges." And then they dropped hints that suggested, perhaps, if you were very good, they might be prepared to reveal the whole character of their proposal.

Sometimes this coyness gets them into trouble. In SALT II, a "new type" missile was defined in part as one that was more than plus or minus 5 percent from an existing missile in certain measures. There was an obscure argument when the Russians came up with a proposal for having a bigger or perhaps no limit on the extent of downsizing changes that could be made, while keeping the five percent limit on increases. We honestly did not know what they were getting at, but we suspected they were up to no good and asked them to explain. They had already agreed to a downward limit. Why were they trying to change? They were unwilling to explain, and we never agreed. To this day, we do not really know what they were trying to get at.

Soviet negotiators are well prepared in a certain, rather legalistic way. That is, they have immensely long memories for minute points. This is especially apparent in the non-arms control areas. They will not only recite the Lenin declaration on peace, but they will also explain how whatever proposal they have just made is really an acceptance of the American–French Initiative of 1954 dealing with the avoidance of something or other. It seems to be a technique of Soviet polemics, this memory for the obscure but embarrassing quotation. They have quoted Harry Truman's foolish remark in 1941 about letting the Russians and the Germans destroy each other countless times in arms control negotiations and elsewhere.

The above-mentioned lessons in cultural characteristics are valid, but there are some "non-lessons" as well, that is, some misperceptions about Soviet attitudes toward negotiations. Occasionally, American observers act shocked that before the Soviet negotiators make major concessions, they must check with the government back home. Admittedly, my experience with this has always essentially been in the position of playing "Venice" to the delegation's "Marco Polo." Still, I had rather hoped the American delegation thought it was under the same obligation.

Certainly, the Soviets usually move slowly. Sometimes it is because they simply have absolutely no interest in reaching an agreement. But some of it is a carry over, both in Soviet practice and in American memory and analysis, from the period of Stalinist terror when negotiators had to be careful of anything they might say in order to survive the next review of party cards. Clearly, on any important matters,

Soviet negotiators cannot do much on their own. But that may not be of great significance. On critical issues in the arms control negotiations, both sides have to check with their capitals. The American negotiators probably have a great deal more de facto flexibility to say things that they are not authorized to say, but the basic proposition is that serious U.S.–Soviet negotiations are not "Marco Polo" operations for either side. The negotiators on both sides are on a very short leash. And when the Soviets want to move things along, they seem quite capable of floating trial balloons, using informal contacts, and the like.

Similarly, the notion that deadlines always work against the United States seems overdone. Of course, if the United States feels itself to be under a deadline and the Soviets are not, that is unfavorable. The United States cannot expect to deal effectively with the Russians in a situation like that. But there is no particular evidence that the United States is at any disadvantage where both sides face a deadline. In the last few weeks of the SALT II negotiations, for example, the Soviets relentlessly broke all of these supposed rules. They put themselves under an earlier deadline than we were, they told us about it, and then they proceeded to make a stream of concessions on a variety of minor technical points. We were able to get some agreements and concessions that they would not normally have given us without weeks and weeks of agonizing debate.[8]

Another supposed rule of Soviet negotiating behavior is that the Soviets expect the Americans to make all the proposals. The record of the INF negotiations — a remarkably complete, contemporary record — shows both sides making many offers. NATO had some fourteen or fifteen different positions, but so did the Soviets. Like the bewildering array of NATO positions on INF, the Russians' positions all had the same basic point, but there were plenty of variations on the theme. It is always easier to react to somebody else's proposal, but there are also dangers in conducting a negotiation that way because it surrenders to the other side the initiative to shape the debate. The record does not indicate that the Soviets are more likely than anyone else to let that happen.

Is it not certain that the Soviet clearance process is, context held constant, any more complicated than that of the Americans. To say that the Politburo has to pass on all SALT proposals is not so shock-

8. See Chapter 5, pp. 51–52 for further discussion of the question of negotiating deadlines.

ing. After all, our current administration, as all previous administrations, regards most SALT issues as sufficiently important to warrant a cabinet-level decision involving the president, and there are frequently substantive disputes that the president has to resolve. The idea that high levels be consulted on critical issues is certainly held by both sides. It may well be that the Soviets have a greater degree of involvement at the top than does the United States. Indeed, they are generally willing to address issues of immense triviality at the top. Presumably this would hold true in arms control negotiations.

Finally, there is the point about "cherry picking," or picking the desirable portions from the other side's proposals and rejecting the rest. Everybody involved in negotiations does some cherry picking, including the Soviets. A concession that is not organically linked to the rest of the points in a proposal will likely be lopped off unless there is some real world reason that makes the concession acceptable only in that context. But that is also a constraint on the Soviets, as it is on anyone else in any negotiations.

I would like to sum up by advancing what I call Harold Brown's law of negotiating with the Russians: When you are negotiating with the Russians, it is not necessary to believe that they are the world's best negotiators who will always get the better of you, but you should at least try to believe that they are not worse negotiators than you are.

8 OBJECTIVES AND NEGOTIATING STRATEGY

Raymond L. Garthoff

Some lessons have been learned from our experience in negotiating with the Soviets, but they have often not been learned by those who need to know them. In general, our government lacks a means of follow-through for what we have learned, so that we must continually relearn old lessons. This unfortunate situation is one of many reasons why it is useful not only to study Soviet negotiating techniques, but also to devote more attention to understanding and improving our own negotiating approach.

Ambassador Jonathan Dean's three categories of motivation for negotiation (see p. 80) provide a very useful point of departure for understanding negotiating approaches: 1) negotiations where it is a matter of indifference as to the outcome or where no agreement is desired, 2) negotiations where there is moderate but no strong or urgent interest in such an outcome, and 3) negotiations where a positive outcome is desired. These categories focus on the issue of whether our aim in a specific negotiation is to reach agreement and, if so, for what broader purpose. It is necessary to settle this question of objective first, before developing strategy, tactics, and techniques for negotiation.

There are respectable alternatives to negotiating for the sake of agreement. We may sometimes pursue a negotiation for reasons of public impact, or we may simply not want to let the other side derive a global public relations advantage from our unreadiness to negotiate. For a negotiation to be successful, it is not necessary to reach an agreement, nor even an informal agreement or better understanding. A negotiation can be a strictly competitive exercise in propaganda and political action.[1]

If, however, there is a strong interest in reaching agreement, it is useful to distinguish between two general categories of goals. These categories can apply to negotiations on any issue, but let us focus on arms control. In some cases, the principal purpose is to achieve one or more arms control restraints. In other cases, agreement may be desired for general political purposes—to contribute to detente, for example. In the early 1970s the Nixon administration did not have a very strong interest in curbing the dynamic of arms competition. But it concluded a successful SALT I agreement for other legitimate reasons. The conclusion of SALT I certainly had a positive effect on U.S.-Soviet political relations. And that was the principal purpose of the negotiation on both sides.

Early in SALT, the main focus switched from negotiating with the Soviets to internal negotiations within the United States. This internal debate was perhaps not a negotiation in the true sense, but rather a determination by the administration to do or not to do certain things. The decision *not* to pursue actively arms control limitations on multiple independently-targetable reentry vehicles (MIRVs) is one dramatic example that illustrates differences in substantive versus political interests as well as short-term versus long-term interests. Short- and long-term arms control interests were not very well balanced in SALT I largely because arms control was not the main purpose of the negotiation. President Nixon and his national security adviser, Dr. Henry Kissinger, cared little about the arms control implications of an ABM treaty coupled with some kind of restraint on the Soviet ICBM build-up versus an ABM treaty coupled with a reciprocal MIRV restraint.

One problem that we have confronted in many negotiations is a lack of unity and consistency in objectives. Perhaps this is inevitable

---

1. Several participants commented on this subject. Some said negotiation is good for its own sake because communication between the superpowers is essential. Others questioned whether negotiations had such independent value, and one insisted that agreement must remain an objective of negotiations. Numerous objectives for negotiations besides agreement or dialogue were advanced. These included exploration, political expediency, and making the Soviet Union more "transparent."

in our system. Certainly, there is a strong tendency to reshuffle and change our objectives, and that is not necessarily bad. In some cases it may be justified, indeed necessary. But as a rule this practice makes it very difficult to design and almost impossible to implement a real negotiating strategy. If the negotiator does not know from the outset what he is trying to accomplish, he cannot very effectively design ways of accomplishing it.

For example, the highest-level preparatory guidance for the preliminary SALT talks in 1969 specifically stated that the United States would retain a nationwide ballistic missile defense against China. Six months later, the same administration changed its position and proposed a National Command Authorities (NCA)-level ABM defense limited to Moscow and Washington. This was before we had even started negotiating with the Soviets. Moreover, that is far from being the only example of such shifts.

In some cases, the leadership has deferred making decisions about our objectives until midway through a negotiation. There are arguments in favor of this approach. One strong argument against it, however, is that it poses tremendous difficulties, both for the negotiator and his superiors, in devising and implementing a negotiating strategy.

The specific objectives one pursues in a negotiation also depend on the degree of one's interest in agreement. For example, if someone is eager to reach an agreement, he is likely to state his requirements for the negotiation in terms that are more negotiable. By contrast, if he is only slightly interested, or not interested, in reaching an agreement, he might as well ask for the moon. In the highly unlikely event that he gets it, he has really gotten something. Otherwise, he has at least gone through the exercise. Such behavior has often been evident in the positions taken by individual elements within the U.S. government. Depending on whether they expected or wanted an agreement, different agencies have sought more or less demanding terms for proposed limitations or for verification of those limitations (apart from real requirements for adequate verification).

In general, we tried in SALT and START to hobble Soviet force developments while preserving our own options. The Soviets have done the same in reverse. Again, this is largely a reflection of each side's basic motivations. If one believes that real arms control constraints are desirable and feasible, then he will be prepared to give up more of his own options in exchange for comparable sacrifices on the other side. But if one is interested in the politically easiest agreement, he will not be prepared to make difficult sacrifices. And if one is not concerned about reaching agreement at all, he will ask for hard concessions on the other side and will refuse to relinquish his own options in exchange. For example, we were not prepared to forego our own MIRV option in SALT I. This problem has little to do with the issue of maintaining a balance; it is possible to maintain a balance either with light sacrifices on both sides or with heavy sacrifices on both sides. The United States — and the Soviet Union — have opted for the light sacrifices.

Certain questions that have been raised about objectives really concern rationales. This has almost always been the case in regard to strategic stability. Granted, most people want strategic stability. But an examination of the record of the arms control constraints that we have pursued in the name of stability shows that stability has more often been a rationale than an objective. Moreover, our definition of stability has changed constantly. At certain times the United States has said that a mobile ICBM would be stabilizing; other times we called it destabilizing. The Soviets have also switched positions. We are the only ones, however, to have reneged, and we have done so on more than one occasion, after the other side has accepted our proposal. We followed a very embarrassing, erratic course on ABM limitations, for example, during the SALT I negotiation. Ambassador Herbert York has given other examples.[2] Such behavior does not encourage reciprocal confidence in the negotiation.

As noted above, the fluidity of our aims makes it extremely difficult to define a strategy. It also causes problems when we try to build in some bargaining room, which is generally a sensible thing to do in negotiations. The fragmentation of aims means that when we concede the bargaining points that were included to pad our position, some elements within the administration, to say nothing of critics outside, charge that the United States is retreating. "Bargaining chips" become part of the stake.

That, incidentally, is one reason for us not to emulate the Soviet negotiating style. The Soviets typically open with an outrageous initial bargaining position and for a time stand firm. But when they do later concede, they tend to make very sweeping concessions. By open-

2. See Chapter 12.

ing with a tough position, they find out as much as possible about U.S. concerns before committing themselves to advancing a fall-back position. This approach works for the Soviets because they can think in terms of multiple fall-backs. We cannot even design one fall-back into our opening position — for several reasons. First, it will be leaked. Second, it will be changed. Third, whereas the Soviets can resort to fall-backs without worrying about being criticized for softness, we do not share that luxury.[3]

Thus fragmented aims have adversely affected our tactics and negotiating techniques. It is hard for the United States to manage tactics effectively because of inconsistent objectives and shifting strategy.

Despite the difficulties in doing so, the United States can do better in setting objectives, devising negotiating strategies, and implementing them in negotiation. Contrary to a widely voiced view, the United States has usually had very capable, tough, and skilled negotiators. In addition, Soviet negotiators and negotiating styles, although also tough and able, are by no means inherently superior. They, too, have problems. If the United States draws the appropriate lessons from its negotiating experience of recent decades and applies them to the pursuit of clear objectives, it can further enhance what is in fact a creditable record.

---

3. One participant noted a dilemma on this point. It is difficult for the delegation to devise a good negotiating strategy if they do not know their fall-back position. But often if they know their fall-back, it will be leaked to the press, undermining their strategy. Another suggested an alternative approach to having a formal fall-back position, one used during the Nixon administration. The idea is to develop for each U.S. arms control option a game plan for acting on possible Soviet responses. A third said that negotiators can never devise a complete game plan in advance but should at least have an idea of their minimum and maximum objectives.

9 EAST–WEST ARMS CONTROL NEGOTIATIONS
The Multilateral Dimension

Jonathan Dean

This chapter describes some lessons learned from the multilateral aspect of East–West arms control negotiations. It focuses on the ten-year experience of the Vienna negotiations for Mutual and Balanced Force Reductions (MBFR) talks, which are prototypal of a coalition pattern of East–West arms control negotiation where, in addition to the United States and the Soviet Union, other members of the opposing NATO and Warsaw Pact alliances participate directly on the respective negotiating teams.

To provide a context for these observations, the chapter begins with some general remarks on arms control negotiations and identifies some specific aspects of U.S.–Soviet behavior in arms control negotiation. It then treats some specific characteristics of multilateral East–West negotiation on arms control as they emerged in the MBFR talks. It reaches the conclusion that the problems of multilateral East–West arms control negotiations are the problems of U.S.–Soviet arms control negotiations writ large, but that this coalition diplomacy has some unexpected benefits. There is all the more reason to examine the lessons of the multilateral East–West format because, from today's perspective at least, it appears improbable that any fully articulated bilateral U.S.–Soviet arms control agreements will actually be concluded in the next four to five years. In that period, multilateral agreements through negotiations of the kind described here or in the Stockholm Conference on Disarmament in Europe (CDE) may be the only ones achievable.

ANALYSIS OF ARMS CONTROL NEGOTIATION

To improve negotiating techniques, we must analyze their role in the total negotiating process. It is useful to analyze East–West arms control negotiation in terms of three main components that interact to determine the success or failure of a given negotiating effort:

1. The degree of interest of the participants in an outcome;
2. The negotiating concepts of the two sides; and
3. Negotiating technique, including the political level at which negotiation is carried out.

The strength of interest shown by one side or the other in bringing about an actual outcome, sometimes called political will, is the decisive element in any East–West arms control negotiation. The degree of political interest in an outcome at any given moment is the product of a complex calculation by national leaderships of domestic and international factors and of the overall East–West relationship. For analytical purposes, interest in outcome of negotiations can be reduced to three major categories:

1. Negotiations where it is a matter of indifference if there is an outcome or where no outcome is desired;
2. Negotiations where there is moderate but not urgent interest in an outcome, but where concessions by the other side or changes in the negotiating environment can intensify interest; and
3. Negotiations where an outcome is actively desired, even at the cost of real negotiating concessions.

Because it involves an overall calculation of how the leadership of each side sees its international position, and because few governments will admit to their negotiating partners or their publics that a given arms control negotiation is not in the top category of their interest and motivation, analysis of political will requires a breadth of information about the motives and perceptions of both sides, which makes it difficult to use without controversy. But, given the central significance of motivation for negotiation, using even these rough categories can have some predictive capacity.

This classification helps to clarify why some specific problems cannot be solved by negotiation at a given time. For example, no negotiation on the sensitive topics of national security that are the subject matter of arms control can be successfully concluded without receiving Category 3 interest at some point from one side or the other. It is probable that in an arms control negotiation where the positive interest of one side is in Category 3, and that of the other side is at least in Category 2, an agreement will be achieved. With the interest of both sides remaining in Category 2, an outcome is improbable; to reach an outcome, the interest of one or the other has to rise to Category 3 at some stage, and the "interest count" has to come to a total of at least five.

Negotiations that fall into Category 1 of interest in an outcome are conducted mainly for the sake of being seen to negotiate. In negotiations where one side has a Category 3 interest but the other has only Category 1 interest, a positive outcome is unlikely. For example, the Soviet Union, motivated by concern over being drawn into a technological race with the United States over ballistic missile defense, probably has a Category 3 interest in concluding a broad agreement banning antisatellite weapons, a subject that has up to now been in Category 1 for the Reagan administration.

For the United States, and probably for the Soviet Union, multilateral arms control negotiations like MBFR, CDE, and the chemical and biological warfare negotiations at the United Nations Conference on Disarmament at Geneva fall into Category 1 or 2 simply because they are considered, rightly or wrongly, not to involve issues of national survival. On the other hand, in the 1970–71 Berlin Quadripartite negotiations, both sides had a Category 3 interest. The Soviets sought to receive the benefits of Federal German ratification of the German detente treaties with the Soviet Union and Poland, which had been linked to conclusion of an acceptable agreement on Berlin. For their part, the United States, the United Kingdom, and France wanted a contractual Soviet guarantee for civilian access to Berlin.

Despite the cardinal importance for any negotiation of intensity of interest in an outcome, the factors affecting intensity of interest are so numerous and varied that this component is in most cases beyond the reach of deliberate change. However, the remaining components of successful negotiation — negotiating concept and negotiating technique — are also in some situations decisive for success or failure of negotiation. And these components can be analyzed and deliberately changed. For these reasons, they will be the focus here, particularly negotiating technique.

As concerns negotiating concept, because experience of the past thirty years warns against expecting far-reaching results from arms control negotiations, most, though not all, American arms control negotiating concepts have reflected fairly modest aims. The United States and Soviet Union now appear so evenly matched in military resources that decisive and enduring superiority for one or the other seems out of the question for the foreseeable future even though individual advantages will continue to exist. And in both the United States and the Soviet Union, the internal dispersal of power and division of opinion over relations with the other superpower among leadership groups make far-reaching concessions by either improbable.

These conditions argue that only those arms control negotiating concepts that adhere to the pattern of limited agreements with a rough balance of concessions between both sides will succeed. If the goal is more ambitious, it will have to be achieved in stages. Despite these limitations, encouraging active creativity in formulating negotiating concepts and in developing alternate solutions for small issues as well as large ones is the single most important action that can be taken to further negotiations where there is active interest in a successful outcome. Above all, negotiators are, or should be, paid to think — to find the formulas that can reconcile conflicting or diverging interests.

With regard to negotiating tactics and methods, the typical arms control negotiation is often visualized as being carried out in some neutral city by officials operating on a fixed negotiating concept formulated in capitals and without authority to change that concept. The object of these officials is to explore the degree of agreement between U.S. and Soviet negotiating positions, to narrow differences where they can, and to refer major areas of difference to higher levels for resolution. Officials in capitals often derrogate the importance of such field negotiation and consequently, of negotiating technique. To them, this core activity of diplomacy has been permanently downgraded by modern telecommunications to an activity of subordinate bureaucracies.

Yet is more accurate to view a given East–West arms control negotiation as a single negotiation conducted at various levels at different times by the negotiators in the field, by secretaries of state and senior officials, and by heads of state and government. Because arms control negotiation involves national security and is controversial in itself, moves that could elicit potentially heavy criticism require personal involvement of top officials on both sides. Without this face-to-face communication at various levels, there could be no negotiated outcome—and negotiating technique is important at all levels. Even if interest in a negotiated outcome is high, governments have to be able to translate their desire to move into specific actions. This is where both imaginative negotiating concepts and negotiating technique come into their own.

There is an unresolved argument between theoreticians and practitioners of negotiation as to the relative importance for negotiating technique of the dynamics of the negotiating process and of cultural factors. The central question is whether the negotiating process follows a standard dynamic with its own rules, or whether the political culture of the negotiators plays a decisive role. Both Soviet/Warsaw Pact and Western negotiators are usually thoroughly familiar with the established repertory of negotiating tactics—for example, presenting starting positions with built-in negotiating "fat," "pocketing" concessions, or insisting that the penultimate concession is the absolute last possible move. Therefore, negotiating theory is useful to the arms control negotiator as a precis of the historical experience, summarizing a range of behavior he may encounter from his negotiating partners. But the characteristics of "socialist" political culture in the Warsaw Pact countries also have a powerful effect on Soviet and Eastern European negotiating behavior. Because "Negotiating Man" sometimes responds in terms of his political culture, and sometimes in terms of negotiating theory, in a varying mix, we must be aware of both.

SOME CHARACTERISTICS OF U.S. AND SOVIET NEGOTIATING BEHAVIOR

Against the background of these general comments, this section describes some characteristic aspects of U.S. and Soviet negotiating behavior in the MBFR talks. Doing so will enable comparison of the MBFR experience with experience in other U.S.–Soviet arms control negotiations. It will also provide some understanding of the negotiating behavior of these two great powers before we turn to the multilateral aspects of arms control negotiations in which their allies participate. It should be said at the outset that it seems probable that many patterns of behavior identified with Soviet negotiating style — rigidity, lack of flexibility, the penchant for secrecy, the insistence on a quid pro quo for every move — may have as much to do with negotiating behavior of all authoritarian systems as with specifically Soviet behavior.

In the MBFR talks and in the day-to-day drafting of the Berlin negotiations as well, even after larger issues had been resolved, Soviet negotiators showed a pronounced tendency to allow or even urge the United States to take the lead and then to react to these leads. Some American critics have claimed, wrongly, that this procedure placed the United States in a position where it had to show all the flexibility by introducing a series of concessions from its own original position, while the Soviets, with greater patience, merely waited to pocket them. This claim was refuted not only in SALT I and II, where the Soviets made by far the larger number of concessions both in number and significance, but in the MBFR negotiations as well, where the Soviet and other Warsaw Pact negotiators moved step by step to accept, at least in principle, the main elements of the Western negotiating approach: (1) the focus on reducing military manpower as distinguished from a focus on reducing armaments and, within this category, on reducing ground force manpower; (2) the idea of reducing military manpower to the same common collective ceiling for both sides; (3) reducing U.S. and Soviet forces first; and (4) most of the associated measures the West has proposed for verifying compliance and reducing the risk of surprise attack, like permanent exit-entry points through which forces entering the Central European reduction area must pass, inspections by forces of the opposing alliance, and prenotification of entry to the area for training or rotation of personnel in large numbers. In return, the only major concession Western participants made in the first ten years of the MBFR talks was to drop their original demand for withdrawal of an entire Soviet tank army (a formation similar to an American armored corps) in the first phase of reductions.

Soviet and other Warsaw Pact negotiators are fairly open with the explanation that their authorities permit them little discretion formally to recommend changes in their own negotiating instructions and that the best way to obtain reaction or change of position from their capitals is for Western negotiators to take the initiative. Once instructions are issued to Soviet or Pact negotiators, there is little opportunity to revise them until the opportunity for oral discussion comes in negotiating recesses. The difficulty of getting instructions from Moscow is one contributory reason for a Soviet tendency to rely on general formulae, with details to be filled in later by subsequent discussion. Pact negotiators seem to have somewhat more latitude in the informal discussions in capitals during recesses. In line with their more rigid guidance and lack of scope for recommending change in the Pact position on their own, Soviet and Pact negotiators seem to do considerably less topical reporting than Western representatives of negotiation developments as they occur, depending more on end-of-round oral summaries.

Understandably, the same factors limit the willingness of Soviet negotiators to explore alternative possibilities without instructions and, like negotiators from the time of antiquity on, to deal with the discouragement of innovative thinking by their authorities. One reason for this phenomenon is that American arms control positions are generally more complex and take into account more factors than Soviet positions, which often call merely for reduction of a limited percentage from existing force levels. But the Soviets have been willing in many cases to approach the American negotiating concept. This requires more movement from them, which they often slice into as many negotiating moves as is logically feasible. Furthermore, the Soviets sometimes resort to the device of ascribing to their Western interlocutors ideas that they themselves may have originated.

As indicated, Soviet negotiators are decidedly close-fisted with their negotiating assets. Not for them the flourish or the generous gesture. They carefully husband negotiating resources, demanding a formal quid pro quo for every move and refusing to go further until NATO participants respond with a move of their own. Even a small Western move may suffice to fulfill the requirements of this rather mechanistic reciprocity, which does not seek to weigh the relative importance of moves made by either side. The underlying attitude is that one does not pitch scarce negotiating resources to the winds or give a bonus to class enemies.

This general approach to agreements is one reason why the concept of acting in the spirit of an agreement is not part of Soviet practice; if a given point is not in the text of the agreement, to follow it nonetheless is an unmerited bonus to Western participants. After the conclusion of the Four-Power Berlin Agreement, the Soviet Union pushed to the limit in attempting to develop implementation favorable to its interpretation in such matters as restricting consular representation by Federal Germany of the interests of West Berliners in Pact countries or the number of Federal German offices established in the Western Sectors. But such behavior is not restricted to the Soviet Union. The Federal Republic did the same thing, moving to establish an environmental office of the European Community in Berlin.

The difference between this Soviet pattern and characteristic American behavior causes problems: The solution-oriented American polity tends to read too much into conclusion of agreements with the Soviets. Americans tend to consider that an agreement, once achieved, marks the end of the problem under discussion, and that the solution will administer itself. With a more accurate view of the ongoing character of East–West relations, the Soviets see implementation of an agreement as a continuing negotiation. And it is true that the implementation of any complicated arms control agreement in changing and developing circumstances requires continual attention from both sides.

The MBFR talks have also been a classic example of the confrontation between American concern with precision and verification and the deep-rooted Soviet preoccupation with secrecy, which Herbert York has described.[1] The insistence of the Western participants that they could not reduce any forces until after the differences between Western and Eastern data on the total number of Warsaw Pact ground and air force personnel in the Central European reduction area had been resolved, and Western proposals that this problem be resolved by increasingly detailed comparison of Western and Eastern data on the Pact forces, elicited Soviet contentions that requests for such detailed information represented Western attempts to obtain sensitive information on Pact armed forces, not for the sake of computing reductions, but for intelligence purposes. In this dispute, Soviet military personnel seemed to be saying that they were the guardians of Soviet military secrets and were not disposed to release them for the purposes of some arms control negotiation. Indeed, in MBFR, as was reported to be the case in the SALT I negotiations, Soviet diplomatic personnel were neither expert nor informed on the details of the

1. Herbert York, "Bilateral Negotiations and the Arms Race," *Scientific American* (October 1983): 149–160.

Warsaw Pact military posture. Successive Soviet delegation heads in MBFR stated that they were wholly uninformed on the subject, and they visibly had to learn on the job.

Soviet negotiators are more disciplined and show less observable tendency than American or Western negotiators to be affected by important events outside the negotiation framework. When the MBFR negotiations began, U.S.–Soviet relations had just been shaken by the 1973 Arab–Israeli war, Soviet moves to resupply the Egyptians, and the U.S. nuclear general alert. Soviet negotiators in Vienna did not mention a single word about any of these subjects. Western negotiators were full of it. The same happened with the 1979 Soviet invasion of Afghanistan and with the repression of Solidarity and imposition of martial law in Poland. One supplementary reason for this is once again secrecy and the way the Soviet system controls the internal dissemination of information. The State Department makes a strong effort to keep its diplomats abroad informed on current issues outside their area of responsibility. In contrast, in the case of Solidarity development, for example, Soviet officials in Vienna received no direct information from Moscow and were dependent on the Polish delegation for news. The result is nearly total compartmentalization of Soviet negotiating behavior and a frustrating lack of clues as to Soviet motivation and thinking.

But Soviet officials probably have an equally difficult time identifying the decisive voices and the many competing American opinions on arms control. For example, in the MBFR talks during both the Nixon and Carter administrations, there was a pattern of repeated leaks of negotiating positions by senior government officials interested in promoting favorable treatment of administration actions by a favored group of White House correspondents. Every major change in the Western negotiating position in MBFR was leaked in this way to the *New York Times,* the *Washington Post,* or the *Los Angeles Times* before it was advanced in Vienna, and often even before it had been raised for discussion with the NATO allies. This behavior pattern greatly mystifies Soviet officials searching for some rational purpose behind repeated violation of the agreed confidentiality of negotiations. There have been fewer leaks in the Reagan administration, but also fewer moves. In any event, the greater role of Congress and public opinion in arms control negotiations brings with it a far greater degree of linkage of even second-rank arms control negotiations with other aspects of East–West relations in American practice than is usual in the authoritarian Soviet system.

Soviet negotiators in the MBFR talks maintained very good self-control except when they considered, rightly, though sometimes quite wrongly, that an effort was being made to pressure the Soviet position or that the Soviet Union was not being given adequate respect as a country. Such suspicions were often accompanied by emotional outbursts (sometimes contrived for tactical impact, but more often quite genuine) to the effect that the Soviet Union was not a defeated power and that it categorically refused to negotiate under ultimatums, and by a high degree of general stubbornness. These reactions seem to reflect a deep-seated feeling of the Soviet system's fragility and of the American system's superiority in many respects. This in turn results in great sensitivity to that Western behavior which is perceived as an effort to treat the Soviets as inferior. Since most Soviet officials, whatever their degree of interest in official ideology, have strong national pride, the reactions described here are fairly frequent.

As often noted in other arms control negotiations, the continuity of the Soviet leadership has also given it a definite advantage over the United States in the MBFR talks. In the first ten years of the Vienna negotiations, the Soviet Union had one political head, Leonid Brezhnev, and one foreign minister, to four American presidents and five secretaries of state. It had one senior foreign ministry official, Vice Minister Kornienko, in charge throughout, in contrast to the United States, where no single official of any level had direct responsibility at any point in the Vienna talks. In the first twelve years of MBFR, there were six U.S. delegation heads, while the Soviets used only three. With every change of U.S. administration, there was a wholesale change of senior Washington personnel with knowledge of the MBFR negotiations, a review of the entire MBFR project, and a six-month hiatus in active negotiation before successive administrations came to the common sense conclusion that it would cost more to withdraw from the negotiations than to continue U.S. participation.

This problem of rapid turnover of American officials at every level is directly related to another pronounced shortcoming in U.S. conduct of arms control negotiations with the Soviet Union, the pernicious tendency to replicate inside the executive branch of the American government the constitutional division of power between the executive, legislative, and judiciary branches. Each agency with interest in arms control has a veto right over the conduct of these negotiations: the National Security Council (NSC), the Department of State, the Arms Control and Disarmament Agency (ACDA), the Department of Defense, the Joint Chiefs of Staff (JCS), and, in practice, the intelligence community, despite the legislative prohibition of a policymaking role for intelligence agencies. The recurrent paralysis induced by this situation is intensified in the case of the Category 1 and 2 negotiations, those which do not receive continual top level interest and attention, by the absence of a single government official with responsibility for moving the negotiations along. In theory, this function could be exercised by the NSC staff. But in most past cases affecting the MBFR negotiations, these officials have been content with the role of preventing interagency dissent over MBFR from adversely affecting the relationship among agency heads or from spilling over to affect interagency consideration of more important issues. As a consequence, the MBFR negotiating delegation in the field has often been without an effective backstop in Washington, and the negotiations have often slumbered in Washington until the delegation has returned during recesses with suggestions for new moves in Vienna.

Most representatives of the agencies participating in coordination of the American position in the MBFR talks, even at a fairly senior level, cannot commit their agencies in the positive sense or take the initiative to recommend some new action, but they do have the capacity to say no and use it often. In this situation, representatives of individual agencies have often suspended onward motion in the Vienna negotiations for a new basic study or questioned the desirability of the negotiations as such. And it is not only a question of negative views. It is a remarkable aspect of a field of activity generally held in as low official repute as negotiation that it shares with politics the quality of effortless, instant expertise, and that anyone who thinks of negotiation for a short time considers himself proficient and an expert. This is particularly the case when negotiations are with a powerful antagonist like the Soviet Union. The prospect of bringing a feared adversary to do your will through the force of your own intellect has irresistible attraction.

By way of comparison, the Soviets have a Defense Ministry-Foreign Ministry coordinating committee for the Vienna talks, but only two agencies, not six, are represented and have a veto. There is evidence in the MBFR talks that the Soviet military were not pleased by the prospect of any agreement, that they blocked at least two proposals for additional data exchange, and that they sat for a long time on the

Western proposals for verification. But the behavior of Soviet military personnel in the MBFR talks has in general been more disciplined and less captious or idiosyncratic than that of the Washington officials discussed here.

Above and beyond these consequences, dispersed authority in Washington has contributed, as in other arms control negotiations, to failure to keep the head of the U.S. delegation adequately informed of developments he needs to know; no one had the clear responsibility to do so. The Nixon-Kissinger administration of foreign policy is known for its secretiveness. This attitude was itself a defensive reaction to the existence of dispersed authority within the U.S. political system, including pluralistic dispersal within the executive branch, with its accompanying phenomenon of the "agency veto." But this protective approach intensified the problem of getting information to the field. The head of the U.S. delegation in the 1973 preparatory talks for the MBFR talks was unaware, during four months of controversy over the status of Hungary which precluded any other business in Vienna, that senior officials in Washington had already indicated to the Soviets tentative agreement to exclude Hungary from the list of active participants. Later, in the Carter administration, even though this information had crucial relevance to the Western position in the talks, a senior Washington official was reprimanded for informing the MBFR delegation of Washington's decision to withdraw the 1975 Western proposal to reduce nuclear weapons in MBFR in order to use these assets in connection with the NATO decision to deploy new intermediate-range nuclear missiles in Europe.

There is usually nothing intentional about this anarchic situation; it is simply sloppy and ineffective. As Herbert York has suggested in his report on the negotiations for a comprehensive test ban (see Chapter 12), this is a situation crying for reform.

Observation of how U.S.–Soviet arms control negotiations have been conducted over the past decade suggests that both the U.S. and the Soviet governments are capable of providing top-level interest and supervision for only one arms control negotiation at a time, and that they not unnaturally give priority to U.S.–Soviet bilateral negotiations that more directly affect their own survival. Throughout the first decade of the MBFR talks, the SALT talks and then the INF negotiations received priority in Washington, and the U.S. position on MBFR was dependent on these talks. Although the U.S. government had agreed in 1972 to make a nuclear reduction offer in MBFR at the proper time, it took two years of intense Washington lobbying to bring the offer about. Senior Washington officials apparently intended to use the presentation of the Western proposal for U.S. nuclear reductions in MBFR to satisfy, at least symbolically, the Soviet interest that American forward-based systems be covered under the SALT agreement. Consequently, the introduction of this proposal to the MBFR talks had to wait until the SALT talks had developed sufficiently.

After the SALT II agreement was signed in 1979, priority attention during the remainder of the Carter administration was given to the emerging NATO two-track decision on theater nuclear forces (TNF, now called INF), which was eventually reached in December of that year. Here again, U.S.–Soviet nuclear negotiation received priority over the Category 2 MBFR talks. In order to smooth the way in NATO for the TNF decision, the 1975 Western proposal in MBFR to reduce American nuclear weapons — Pershing 1 missiles, F-4 aircraft, and nuclear warheads — was withdrawn. The modernized Pershings were shifted to the TNF negotiations, and it was decided that the United States should unilaterally withdraw the thousand nuclear warheads previously offered in MBFR.

For their part, the Soviets showed they had the same priority of arms control interests — U.S.–Soviet nuclear issues first. In his October 1979 speech in East Berlin, in the effort to persuade European NATO members to reject the TNF decision and deployment of the American Pershing 2's and ground-launched cruise missiles, Brezhnev announced the unilateral withdrawal of 20,000 Soviet troops from East Germany. These were the same forces that the Soviets had at the beginning of 1979 offered to withdraw in a first MBFR agreement providing for limited U.S.–Soviet reductions, which they proposed be concluded at the time of the signature of SALT II in summer 1979. Perhaps the fairly atypical unilateral gesture also reflected internal Soviet requirements to reorganize and beef up Soviet ground forces remaining in Central Europe. But in any event, without saying it explicitly, both sides were withdrawing their negotiating chips from the MBFR talks to transfer them to a U.S.–Soviet nuclear negotiation to which each attached higher priority.

MULTILATERAL NEGOTIATION

Multilateral configuration of East–West arms control negotiations magnifies the difficulties of the bilateral forum by 200–500 percent, depending on how the expanded participation is organized. This is because, as a representative of a sovereign country, each Western delegate has a right to veto, paralleling in a more formal sense the situation among the participating agencies in Washington. Where negotiation is among a coalition of allies, as in the MBFR negotiations, and it has been agreed — this is important — that the coalition should act together and have a single position, then the coalition cannot make the slightest move in negotiation, cannot make a single statement, without agreement of all participants. On the Western side, a coalition negotiation is a confederation in action. Given the more dominant position of the Soviet Union within the Warsaw Pact and the relative weakness of restrictions on its decisionmaking power stemming from the presence of allies, the difficulty of reaching decisions within the Warsaw Pact alliance is not identical. Nonetheless, it is similar in terms of the requirement of additional time for coordination of positions among governments.

If we compute the time an American MBFR negotiator spends in consultation with his own capital by telegram, phone, and in person at 30 percent of his total working time and estimate that 25 percent of his time is spent in coordination with his own delegation, the requirements of coalition diplomacy amount to about 40 percent of his time. Only 5 percent or less remains for negotiating contacts of all kinds with representatives of the Warsaw Pact or for creative reflection.

The practical problems of multilateral negotiation are in essence the problems of multi-agency confederation in Washington writ large. Everyone wants to get into the action with the Soviet Union and its allies, and everyone, both the allied negotiator and his capital, has different ideas on how to go about it. Many steps were taken to meet these desires, resulting in considerable procedural complexity. But it should be said at the outset of this discussion of multilateral practices that these practices served serious aims as well as sometimes frivolous ones. At the commencement of the MBFR talks, U.S. and NATO negotiators had in mind Soviet efforts of the 1950s to divide the Western allies and were intent on taking all necessary measures to ensure cohesion of the allies in a negotiation that many feared would provide the Soviets with wide opportunity for divisive tactics. U.S. officials also wanted the U.S. delegation to be in a position to exercise a leadership role in the proceedings through close coordination. (A third, political objective was to head off the pressures for unnegotiated, unilateral force reductions on the part of the United States and of several European NATO countries.) Though costs in time-consuming procedures were high, these objectives were for the most part met.

In the early stages of American and Western planning on the MBFR talks, it was intended that only those NATO countries with military forces located in the western part of the NATO "guidelines area," comprised of the territory of the Federal Republic of Germany, Belgium, the Netherlands, and Luxembourg, would participate in the talks. (France refused to participate.) This concept would have resulted in a Western negotiating coalition comprised of seven allied countries: Belgium, Canada, the Netherlands, Luxembourg, the Federal Republic of Germany, the United Kingdom, and the United States. It was planned that these NATO countries would negotiate with the four Warsaw Pact countries — the Soviet Union, Czechoslovakia, Poland, and the German Democratic Republic (G.D.R.) — that had forces on the territory of the eastern three states. Other NATO members could follow the proceedings from Brussels, making whatever comment on the proceedings they wished at NATO.

But Italy and especially Turkey pressed very hard for participation in Vienna. As a result, the MBFR negotiations acquired five additional NATO "flank" participants: Italy, Greece, and Turkey from the southern flank, and Norway and Denmark from the northern flank. The number of NATO participants had nearly doubled. To strike a balance, the NATO participants invited the remaining member states of the Warsaw Pact: Hungary, Rumania, and Bulgaria.

Initially, American officials thought of the flank representatives in Vienna, or "special" participant states, as observers who would watch the proceedings and report back to their home governments. But the idea of selecting only a few NATO members as intermediaries and leaving the others out of the discussion with the Soviets caused great difficulties of national status. At one point in the preparatory talks, the Belgian representative walked out of the NATO Ad Hoc group protesting excessive use of emissaries in place of plenary sessions in which all countries would participate. Also, the Warsaw Pact Rumanian representative threatened to resign if all negotiation was not carried out in plenary sessions rather than by emissaries. Italy took a similar viewpoint, wishing to eliminate procedural distinctions between special and direct participants to the maximum possible.

Provisional solution of the issue of Hungary's status finally opened the road to holding plenary sessions in Vienna, and attention turned to formulating an agenda for the MBFR negotiations proper. But the problems of alliance coordination continued. From the NATO viewpoint, each Western statement in plenary session was to be a previously agreed statement representing the corporate alliance view. Such statements obviously had to be prepared and approved in advance. Consequently, there could be no genuine impromptu discussion in plenary sessions. Clearly, there was a need for a smaller forum where some degree of informal discussion would be possible on the understanding that it would not be binding for the alliance. But who should participate in these smaller groups? Italy and other flank states refused to agree to a system of informal sessions in which all direct participants from both sides would participate — on the grounds that this procedure would document a distinction in status between direct and special participants. But if not all direct participants were to go to informal sessions, who should be excluded?

It took many weeks of internal discussion before a procedure was agreed upon. Three of the Western direct participant countries — the United States plus two delegation heads from remaining NATO direct participants on a rotating basis — would attend each session. The Soviets, mystified, agreed to cooperate in this format, although it meant leaving out one direct participant on their side from each session and caused friction for them. Later in the negotiations, the NATO flank participants insisted not only on receiving a full report of the informal sessions, but also on approving in advance what Western representatives said at these sessions, making these sessions, which originally saw a good deal of free discussion, routinized as well. NATO special participants also subsequently effectively claimed the right for themselves to participate in approving the content of plenary statements by NATO direct participants. Thus, although these special participants would not be reducing their forces under an agreement and perhaps not undertaking any obligations at all, they participated fully in determining Western tactics and statements.

Yet the objective of gaining greater status and control for NATO flank participants was partially frustrated. Much informal discussion was driven into bilateral talks with Warsaw Pact representatives. These, it is true, were regularly reported to the Ad Hoc Group of NATO delegation heads, but many of the more interesting points were initially saved for home reporting. And as the alliance coordination structure became more articulated and moved more slowly, a parallel system of coordination and consultation by a smaller group emerged on the Western side. Inspired by years of successful coordination of Berlin and German issues, the Federal Republic, the United Kingdom, and the United States from time to time informally coordinated their positions in meetings of their negotiators in Vienna and of senior officials in capitals. Like the inner group of the informals and like every inner group, the existence of these trilateral meetings, sometimes indiscretely publicized, caused some resentment and friction with nonparticipating allies.

Meanwhile, at NATO headquarters in Brussels, there was a parallel proliferation of institutions motivated by the same desire to get a bigger piece of the action. In order to give the NATO Council an active role, it was decided that the Council should determine "strategic" guidance for the Ad Hoc Group in Vienna, although it would have been feasible to coordinate instructions from national capitals in Vienna as is done in the Stockholm CDE talks at the insistence of France. But NATO permanent representatives in Brussels found it impossible to cope with all the details of the talks themselves, so their deputies and political counselors, organized as the Senior Political Committee (SPC), were called on to deal with the problem. This additional apparatus would not have created serious problems had the Vienna talks progressed fairly rapidly. But from 1975 on, the talks bogged down in the data dispute—the argument between East and West on the number of Warsaw Pact military personnel in Central Europe—mentioned above. As the talks slowed to a standstill, the SPC gradually broadened the scope of its guidance to the Ad Hoc Group, taking over many tactical details. And, also in Brussels, a special MBFR Working Group was formed of military officers and defense experts to make technical studies. The group was designed, as one European official stated, to assure that the United States did not have things all its own way and move the Vienna negotiations too rapidly (sic).[2]

Prior to the start of the MBFR negotiations proper on October 30, 1973, the NATO Council codified these practices in a charter for the Ad Hoc Group. According to this charter of procedures and the practices that grew up around it, a new concept or idea would go through

2. A participant argued that close on-site coordination among NATO allies in a multilateral negotiation was not necessary as long as coordination was good in Brussels. He said the benefits of alliance cohesion were achieved in the INF and CDE talks without requiring cumbersome on-site coordination. Another added that a serious negotiation in which allies' interests are involved requires good coordination in Brussels.

some twelve stages before being put forward in a plenary session in Vienna to Warsaw Pact participants. If originated in Washington by one government agency, it might be discussed in various versions in several sessions of the interagency coordinating group and sometimes the National Security Council. It would then sometimes be discussed in a trilateral session with British and Federal German officials and sometimes returned to capitals for further work. Next it was introduced into the NATO Council and developed further in the Special Political Committee, often with participation of experts from capitals and with evaluations from Supreme Headquarters Allied Powers, Europe (SHAPE), the MBFR Working Group, or the NATO Military Committee.

The idea would then be sent to the Ad Hoc Group in Vienna as instructions or guidance for the Group. There, it would often be discussed trilaterally and then in the Ad Hoc Group. The Group would normally authorize the U.S. delegation to give a preview to the Soviet delegation, and the proposal would be advanced in an East–West informal session and finally in a plenary session. Each of these twelve steps involved intensive exposition, discussion, adjustment of texts, and so on. The process has been executed more rapidly on occasion, but on the average, a limited initiative would take two months from beginning to end of the process and a more complicated one, four to six months, with the bulk of the time spent in NATO consultation. Counting officials who participate in capitals, at NATO, on military staffs, and at Vienna, a total of 200 to 300 officials of 12 NATO governments, most of whom have at least veto power, must pass on each move made by Western negotiators at Vienna. About fifty officials of NATO countries have to pass on each word spoken to Eastern negotiators in plenary and informal sessions.

In an East–West arms control negotiation conducted on a coalition basis, there is little possibility of maintaining confidentiality of the Western position from the Warsaw Pact negotiators. Pact intelligence penetration of individual NATO members countries, especially of the NATO apparatus, is considerable, as has been repeatedly revealed over the past decade. And with hundreds of officials in Vienna and capitals discussing the MBFR negotiations with representatives of Warsaw Pact states, many details are revealed through indiscretion or lack of knowledge about precisely which aspects of the Western position have been revealed to the Pact by NATO negotiators in Vienna.

Beyond this is the classic motive force of diplomatic discourse: The weakest point in the psychology of the government official, Western or Eastern, is his fear of being considered ignorant in his own field of professional expertise, of not being in the know on his government's decisions. Most experts derive their greatest satisfaction from demonstrating this knowledge to a fellow practitioner, thereby gaining acknowledgement of their professional capacity and new knowledge through trading indiscretions. Added to these confidentiality difficulties is the problem of press leaks in Western democracies, whose frequency is multiplied by the number of participating states. All of these considerations make it necessary, in multilateral East–West arms control negotiations, to adopt a relatively open and direct style of negotiation, relying on repetition and emphasis to get across important points and relinquishing the advantages of confidentiality.

It is evident that differences among national positions on issues of substance and among individual countries' degrees of interest in achieving a negotiated outcome complicate multilateral East–West arms control negotiation. The desire of the Turkish government to achieve maximum representation in the MBFR negotiations, perhaps the crucial element in increasing the number of NATO participants, derived from the Turkish desire to be a signatory of a possible MBFR agreement. This desire in turn reflected the long-term policy of the Turkish government since the time of Kemal Ataturk to be considered a Western country, fully participating in the complex of European affairs. Italy's push for participation at Vienna and for maximum standing seemed to reflect considerations of national prestige characteristic of Italian international behavior, rather than interest in the subject matter, even as concerns the impact on the flank states of possible reductions of NATO forces in Central Europe. Rather, once their status had been established, the Italians played a hypercritical and skeptical role in the Vienna talks, consistently questioning the premises and emphasizing the potential risks of each NATO move.

Federal German sensitivity to the idea of inspection of German forces by Soviet forces — motivated mainly by rejection of control of West German forces by the Soviet Union — for years delayed the presentation in Vienna of a Western proposal providing for mutual inspection of Pact and NATO forces. Eventually the F.R.G. came to see the advantages of a mutual gain in security as outweighing these considerations, understandable as they were. Federal German antipathy to the idea of individual national ceilings on German forces imposed by a treaty with the Soviet Union, driven in part by a determination to avoid a parallel to the Versailles experience, resulted in persistent German insistence that the residual ceilings imposed on military manpower of each alliance after reductions be collective in nature. The F.R.G. took this position despite the fact that it weakened the allied case for an individual national ceiling on Soviet forces remaining in the area after reductions.

Changes in national governments during the negotiations brought changes in national positions at the Vienna talks. At the beginning of the MBFR negotiations, Federal Germany was so interested in an outcome that, for a time, it insisted on being included in reductions from the outset rather than waiting for a second phase of negotiation to make its reductions. Germany was dissuaded only by American arguments that simultaneous reduction of European NATO forces along with American forces would not be an effective means of dealing with domestic pressures for force reductions in the United States.

Later, with the change from the Brandt–Scheel government to the Schmidt–Genscher government, differences of view between the latter two leaders tended to neutralize the German contribution to MBFR. On one occasion, Chancellor Helmut Schmidt attempted to resolve a major impasse of the MBFR talks over limitations on national forces under an alliance-wide collective ceiling for NATO and the Pact by suggesting that no single participant in either alliance should have more than 50 percent of the manpower of its side, a rule that would in practice have imposed some sub-limit only on Soviet and Federal German forces in the Central European reduction area, and thereby resolved one of the principal negotiating impasses. But Foreign Minister Hans-Dietrich Genscher's opposition to this proposal by the head of his own government caused it to be dropped. Still later, the Federal German defense ministry, faced with the problem of coping with a reduced flow of conscripts because of a decline in the Federal German birthrate, became a more enthusiastic proponent of achieving an MBFR agreement than the German Foreign Ministry. Marked changes in the British approach to the MBFR talks, from cool to positive and again to cool, accompanied the shift from the Heath to the Callaghan to the Thatcher governments.[3]

---

3. One participant suggested that allied unity was not as essential in MBFR as in the INF talks because only in the latter case were the British and Germans pushing hard for an agreement.

The French position on MBFR merits comment in this discussion of the effects on MBFR of divergent national policies. Despite repeated American, Soviet, and Federal German efforts to persuade France to participate in MBFR, France refused to do so on the ground that MBFR agreements if achieved would create a special regime in a special zone in Europe, a regime that might ultimately lead to the weakening of Federal German ties with NATO and the neutralization of Germany. The best way for France to prevent this improbable outcome would have been to participate in the Vienna negotiations. But France had left the NATO integrated military command in 1966 because of its excessive restrictions on the exercise of French sovereignty and apparently feared that the tight coordination of coalition diplomacy would mark too close a return to this earlier status. Instead, it used its continued membership in the alliance and its presence at sessions of the NATO Council to prevent any infringement by MBFR on its interests. One result was a six-month delay in active negotiation in Vienna in 1975, when France, which had in 1973 permitted NATO to include in its data covering NATO forces in Central Europe figures on the numbers of French forces in Federal Germany, refused to permit their inclusion in an update of NATO data.

SOME BENEFITS OF COALITION DIPLOMACY

The difficulties of coalition negotiation on the MBFR pattern, with the requirement for agreeing on totally uniform Western statements from numerous participants with widely divergent views on tactics and substance, are enormous. This realization makes easier to understand why an agreement has not been achieved in Vienna during the past decade; indeed, it is something of a miracle that well over half the items needed for a modest first agreement have been agreed. (Points of agreement are mentioned above in the discussion of Soviet tactics and in the author's article, "MBFR, From Apathy to Accord.")[4]

Despite the difficulties that have made it a cautionary example for negotiators, the multilateral format in MBFR has had many benefits for Western participants. The pattern of alliance relationships among the NATO members as embodied in the consultative procedures of

4. Jonathan Dean, "MBFR: From Apathy to Accord," *International Security,* Vol. 7, no. 4 (Spring 1983): 116–139.

the Ad Hoc Group gave even the smallest NATO participant, at least in theory, the same chance as the United States to contribute to the formation of joint NATO positions. In actual practice, it did ensure each NATO representative's full right to be heard. From the outset of the talks, Eastern European negotiators observed with surprise and close attention the pattern of relationships within the group of NATO participants, so different from the Pact relationship. And subsequently, they engineered the establishment of similar mechanisms of coordination on the Warsaw Pact side. Such institutions are not of great consequence for the overall structure of Soviet relations with the Eastern European countries, but, over the years, several hundred Pact officials have moved on to other jobs and spread the word about the Vienna situation.

For the West, the close and structured coordination of the MBFR talks — in capitals, Brussels, and Vienna — provides an element of continuity that compensates for frequent turnover of U.S. and other officials. The sometimes exasperating detail of alliance consultation has provided more careful assessment of the risks and dangers of possible Western moves. After the long debates in the Ad Hoc Group, Western negotiators have generally been better prepared for discussion of specific issues than Warsaw Pact representatives.

With all its leaks and ego-gratifying revelations of recent alliance thinking, the multilateral process has also produced more information about the considerations underlying Pact moves than normally comes out of bilateral negotiation with Soviet participants; the Soviet Union must, after all, explain and justify its proposed moves to its allies in rational terms. Above all, in enabling relatively uncontrollable speculative discussion between representatives of both sides, the multilateral process has provided a medium where new approaches can be discussed without attracting penalties or being given excessive weight. The considerably greater difficulty of promoting such discussion in bilateral U.S.-Soviet arms control negotiations makes this aspect very important. In the multilateral setting, if a Western negotiator finds it difficult to have "what if" discussions with the Soviet representative and considers some other Pact representative a more discerning conversation partner, then he can also be sure that a summary of his ideas will be passed along for discussion in the Warsaw Pact consultations.

As we have seen, coalition diplomacy in MBFR imposes a need for exhaustive discussion at each stage of all possible outcomes. The opportunity this discussion presents for full input by all participants (an input visible to the home publics of participating NATO members) and the important opportunity of having first-hand experience with the Soviet position have engendered great cohesion among NATO members. This has been true even when their attitudes toward the negotiation itself clearly diverged. These circumstances have also brought visibly shared responsibility for the conduct of the talks, an element that has been sorely missing in the bilateral U.S.-Soviet INF talks, even though the NATO mechanism for policy input of member states in INF has worked satisfactorily. Finally, over the years of the Vienna talks, there have been benefits from the opportunity for quiet, non-polemical East-West discussion of the force posture and strategy of both sides, benefits not found as commonly in bilateral superpower talks. This alone makes an important contribution to reducing misperceptions.[5]

CONCLUSIONS

Of the three components of successful negotiation identified at the outset of this chapter—interest in a negotiated outcome, a carefully crafted negotiating concept, and skillful negotiating tactics—the first is indisputably the most important. But, as the product of the general situation, it is not readily subject to improvement by change in institutions or procedures. The other two elements, negotiating concept and negotiating tactics, are both susceptible to systematic change.

The formulation of negotiating concepts in terms of a desired outcome is a proper subject of analysis in any effort to improve negotiation techniques. Even more than is generally the case in negotiation, Western arms control negotiating concepts, once advanced to Pact negotiators, tend to be cast in concrete and difficult to retreat from. Consequently, more care, imagination, and attention should be paid to the formulation of these concepts. The MBFR objective of equality in military manpower between NATO and the Warsaw Pact made sense in the NATO preparations for MBFR, when the Pact was seen as having a superiority of 35,000 men over NATO in the Central Euro-

5. Other benefits of alliance coordination in a multilateral negotiation were cited. One speaker said that such collective work could improve a U.S. proposal, as well as educate NATO and European foreign ministry officials. Another suggested that greater inclusion of allies in the arms control process would facilitate better coordination on NATO force planning.

pean Reduction Area. It became harder to achieve when NATO subsequently estimated Pact superiority at 180,000 ground force personnel. But the NATO common ceiling concept remained unchanged.

In those cases where American administrations want to have real results from arms control negotiations, it will be important for top decisionmakers — the president and the secretary of state — to give more direct attention than usual to the negotiating concept in the formative stage. Many negotiating concepts give insufficient weight in their formulation to what is known about Soviet positions, focusing instead on a description of American desiderata. Forecasts of Soviet reactions by experts are often rejected as speculative. And often they are, especially if the subject matter has not been negotiated on earlier.

In such cases, it would be worthwhile to have one or more exploratory sessions with Soviet representatives for an informal, non-binding exchange of views before settling on an American negotiating concept.[6] We might get a better idea of the Soviet posture and they of ours, and there would be better evidence on which to base the U.S. or Western negotiation concept. On another point, the U.S. negotiator should be brought into the formulation of the U.S. negotiating concept at the outset. He will have to defend and present it, so he should know its genesis in detail. This is sometimes done but is not standard practice. Often negotiators are appointed just as formal negotiation is about to begin.

Something must be done about the near anarchy among U.S. agencies in the coordination of U.S. positions on arms control. The situation calls for serious structural reform in the future. For the moment, I have three practical suggestions. First, it should not be open to an individual agency, once an administration has decided to enter an arms control negotiation and a basic position has been developed, to initiate restudy of the basic desirability of the negotiation, as occurred more than once in MBFR quite apart from reviews at the beginning of new administrations.

Second, given the departmental structure of the American government, it is necessary for agency heads to have the right to object to the president on negotiation moves of which they fundamentally disapprove. But once an interagency negotiating position has been hammered out and negotiations are in progress, this right should be restricted solely to agency heads or their immediate deputies rather than

---

6. Much discussion focused on the problem of formulating an opening position. Exploratory sessions are one way of dealing with this problem. See Chapter 5, pp. 52–53.

placed at the disposal of subordinate officials more disposed to enjoy interagency conflict. A limitation of this kind would oblige agency officials to brief an agency head on the disputed issue and to convince him that the subject is worth contesting at a senior level. This requirement would eliminate obstructionism on petty issues. True, it might at times result in stasis at the head of agency level, but at least the president will have the evidence of deadlock before his own eyes and be able to act on a specific issue, rather than having to try to kick an entire balky bureaucracy into action.

Third, experience indicates that both the American and Soviet governments can give priority attention to only one East–West arms control negotiation at a time. This does not mean negotiating on only one subject at a time. But it is a fact that only continuous top-level attention, with continuous encouragement by agency heads, can move any project through the U.S. government. If, while giving priority to a given arms control negotiation, an American administration wants to move a second project forward, it should fix overall responsibility for doing so on a single, clearly identified senior official who has some direct access to the president (perhaps in the form of ad hoc participation in sessions of the NSC devoted to the negotiations in question) and should make it possible for him to spend a good deal of time on it. With due account of troubled past relationships between the president's national security advisers and secretaries of state, the best place for such an official is probably on the NSC staff. There he would have some access to the president and could use the authority of this link to deal with divergences in agency positions, in particular counteracting the excessive weight of the Department of Defense. Assistant secretaries who devote few hours per week or month in their busy schedules to chairing a coordinating session or preparing for it, and who have many other priority operational issues to deal with, are no substitute for such a designated official.[7]

On a more general plane, administrations that want results in a given arms control negotiation should keep in mind that East–West arms control negotiation is a hostage to fortune, exposed to all kinds of setbacks from external events. In a difficult relationship like the U.S.–Soviet relationship, it must be anticipated that most external events will be negative ones: discovery of a Soviet combat brigade in Cuba, Soviet invasion of Czechoslovakia and Afghanistan, the September 1983 shooting down of the Korean airliner, or mistreatment

7. See Chapter 12, especially footnote 1, for more discussion of this issue.

of Andrei Sakharov and other dissidents. The longer any negotiation continues, the higher the possibility of such negative developments. A related factor is the rather short-term nature of the American presidential election cycle. In practical terms, these factors mean that slow, steady progress in an East–West arms control negotiation that is of Category 3 interest to the United States is not sufficient. Instead, a deliberate high-level effort must be made to maintain negotiating momentum and to accelerate the normal pace of decisionmaking on both sides, even if this to some degree entails deliberately imposed deadlines.

At the same time, there is a place for the structured East–West dialogue on security issues, which has been one of the benefits of the MFBR talks (in other words, the gain from the negotiating *process* as such, aside from negotiating *results*). Such dialogue risks becoming polemical if it is severed from the negotiation process or if the sole purpose of the process is dialogue. Nonetheless, there is a serious need, particularly in a time of strained U.S.–Soviet relations, for systematic, institutionalized U.S.–Soviet and East–West discussion on security issues. One way this could be provided for is to give the MBFR or CDE talks a parallel function as a discussion center on military affairs, with an East–West steering committee that could call on senior military officers and defense officials of both alliances to talk on designated subjects. Results from a multilateral effort would probably be better than a U.S.–Soviet effort to do the same thing, even if U.S.–Soviet relations were better than they now are. A second function that could be usefully superimposed onto the Vienna talks is that of a NATO–Warsaw Pact crisis management center.

Any given problem in arms control negotiations usually has several potential solutions. The more difficult part of the process is not to conceive of possible conceptual solutions, but to conceive of those solutions that can command wide political support, first on one side, and then on the other. Difficult as it is to provide for this institutionally, there is a real need for more creative thinking in arms control negotiations. In an effort to gain some of the benefits of speculative discussion that come with the multilateral framework, it should be possible to attach a planning officer to each American delegation engaged in bilateral U.S.–Soviet arms control negotiation whose recognized function, right, and duty would be to question established policy and practice in the positions of both sides. The Soviets might in due course be persuaded to designate a similar official. This action has been taken from time to time in past negotiations, but it should be made standard procedure.

Finally, this chapter has described the benefits for alliance cohesion of direct participation in East–West arms control negotiations by our Western European allies. Through direct participation, the allies can assure themselves that their views are being fairly and forcefully represented to the Soviet Union and can directly observe the Soviet reaction to Western proposals. They can personally test the firmness of the Soviet position on a given issue. They are not dependent on an American official for an account of these developments – all members of the alliance have the same experience. And all member governments are directly observed by their publics to have some share in responsibility for the outcome of the negotiations.

The desire of officials of the Carter and Reagan administrations to avoid the extra price of direct participation by NATO allies in the INF negotiations is understandable. In my view, however, these costs would not have been as high as the political damage the United States has incurred in decline of public support for U.S. leadership in Europe by conducting the INF talks as bilateral U.S.–Soviet talks.[8] The trick is to work out some system that provides most of the benefits of multilateral participation as described here, yet avoids the high costs of total coordination experienced in the MBFR talks.

We should in any event pay the extra price and bring Western European allies directly into U.S.–Soviet negotiation on nuclear weapons in the resumed talks on INF, through establishment of a working group on intermediate and tactical nuclear armaments, which would be expected to negotiate on this subject matter as a NATO team with the Soviet Union and its Warsaw Pact allies. If necessary, a selective delegation principle like that used in the NATO Nuclear Planning Group or the MBFR informals, or representation on the basis of actual deployment of American nuclear weapons on the territory of the country involved, can be used to keep the number of participants

8. Mr. Dean added that having the allies at a negotiating table forces them to stick to the allied position, once it is agreed upon. Another participant disagreed that it would have been desirable to have the allies at the INF table. He argued that such an allied role would have been counterproductive because the allies resisted direct participation and because it would have led to the inclusion of tactical nuclear weapons based on allied soil, a development that would have made agreement even more difficult. He added that alliance cohesion was so important in INF that the allies had an effective lever to affect the substance and pace of the negotiating, while the United States had to take ultimate responsibility for the position.

at a workable level. An alternative is to move negotiation on INF and shorter-range nuclear weapons in Europe into the MBFR framework, which already provides for direct participation of Western and Eastern Europeans. The French can stay home if they wish, with some provision made for taking account of their assets.

But to maintain long-term cohesion in the NATO alliance, we should move toward a principle whereby all nuclear weapons capable of hitting any part of the territory of either alliance are covered in East–West arms control negotiations with direct European participation. Whatever subceilings or warhead counting system may be used, or whatever arrangements made to take account of U.S. and Soviet Asian defense needs, the principle of shared risk of nuclear destruction requires some form of direct European participation in all East–West negotiations on arms control in Europe, including those on limiting nuclear weapons.

10 REFLECTIONS ON THE MADRID CSCE REVIEW CONFERENCE

Max M. Kampelman

When I went to Madrid to negotiate at the Conference on Security and Cooperation in Europe (CSCE) Review Conference, I went with little formal diplomatic experience, but with extensive experience as a negotiating lawyer in the American private sector. I had, of course, detailed knowledge of the political process in the United States, and I had been a student of the Soviet Union for several decades. Nonetheless, I undertook a good deal of pre-conference preparation.

It quickly became clear to me that there were three kinds of support problems, which reflected three different (if related) constituencies to which I was responsible. Accordingly, an important part of our preparation was to establish the necessary constituencies and support groups before the Madrid meetings. These efforts, perhaps thought by some to be extraneous to the negotiating process, in fact allowed us to have what success we did at the Madrid Review Conference.

The first constituency, and the first set of support problems, involved the U.S. government and particularly the Department of State. I exerted much effort to become acquainted with State Department personnel and with key figures in the National Security Council, the Department of Defense, and the Arms Control and Disarmament Agency, and I tried to learn their sense of what our major problems at Madrid would be. This process, begun at the very beginning of my stewardship, is one I continued vigorously throughout the three years of the review conference. Clausewitz's first principle, to secure one's base, seems as true of diplomacy as of warfare.

But beyond the U.S. government, I believed I needed a domestic constituency in the American public to support our work at Madrid. Ethnic and human rights groups tended to be skeptical of government officials and their "promises." I was aware of that. Nurturing this constituency was made easier by the existence of the CSCE Commission. The commission, a unique governmental agency established by law, includes members of both houses of Congress as well as representatives from the State, Commerce, and Defense Departments. It is concerned on a full-time basis with the complete range of CSCE substantive issues, and particularly with human rights. The commission was able to supply most of the detailed information I needed, except in the case of security issues, where the key data remained in the executive branch agencies. Moreover, the commission alerted me to its extensive network of private and independent sector contacts throughout the United States, voluntary organizations and other institutions concerned about one or another aspect of the Helsinki Final Act. Before the Madrid meeting opened in September 1980, I visited about a dozen U.S. cities to meet with ethnic groups and human rights organizations interested in the CSCE review process.

During the CSCE Review Conference itself, I kept in touch with the extensive list of concerned individuals and organizations brought to the surface by these pre-Madrid meetings, forwarding to them copies of our delegation's speeches and regular updates on what was transpiring at the conference. Over time, skepticism about the ability of the delegation to advance the views and concerns of these groups began to fade. The net result was that these groups, heretofore cynical about the willingness or capacity of the U.S. government to speak to their concerns, became some of our strongest domestic supporters. All of this was greatly aided by the presence in Madrid of forty "public members" appointed by President Carter, who served from the conference opening in November 1980 through its first phase, which ended at Christmas. These "public members" were drawn largely from groups with ethnic and human rights concerns.

The third constituency whose support was essential was comprised of our European allies. I was determined to avoid alliance divisiveness wherever possible. To that end, the Department of State arranged for me an extensive set of meetings in Europe prior to the Madrid conference. Our allies went out of their way to be cooperative and introduced me to numerous high-level officials — foreign ministers and even heads of governments — in addition to my CSCE counterparts. It was clear that the Europeans took the CSCE Review Conference more seriously than did our own government, which then tended to view CSCE as a necessary, but unimportant, sideshow. Paradoxically, that attitude allowed me considerable freedom to chart my own course.

The sensitivity of these exchanges with allies is illustrated by our pre-Madrid discussions regarding "naming names" of particular Soviet and East European dissidents. Should we or should we not be this specific at the actual review conference? Ambassador Arthur Goldberg's experience at Belgrade on this question had been less than optimal. The president undoubtedly wanted him to deal actively with the question of Soviet dissidents; the State Department, I was told, did not want names named, nor did the allies. When Ambassador Goldberg actually cited six cases by name, he was criticized, despite the fact that he was carrying out the president's wishes and was doing so with great skill. In an effort to avoid such confusion and consternation, I raised the question of naming names whenever I met with European counterparts prior to the Madrid meeting. At these encounters, I said that my personal inclination was to be specific; I was a lawyer, and to argue a case persuasively, I had to be able to illustrate the case with names. (The Department of State by now supported me fully in this position.)

Not all of our allies shared my inclination, however. For instance, Bonn told us that the Federal Republic of Germany could not go along with the policy of naming names. During the previous year (1979), the West Germans had managed to get some 49,000 ethnic Germans released from the East — not with petitions or demonstrations, not with picket signs in front of the Soviet Embassy, but with quiet diplomacy. Not surprisingly, and quite understandably, they did not want to jeopardize continued success at repatriation. I told our German allies that I fully understood their position and did not want to be responsible for one person left behind the Iron Curtain who might otherwise be released. Still, I maintained, we did not have to see our two approaches as opposed; they could be complementary. I suggested that we in the West view ourselves as an orchestra in which some musicians are required loudly to bang drums and blow the trumpets, while others play softly on the harp or muted strings. Moreover, as in some orchestras, one person could at times play different instruments. What was crucial, I emphasized, was that we make music together and that there be harmony in our work. This became the key and the theme of U.S.-allied cooperation at Madrid.

Solidifying these three above-mentioned bases of support did not conclude our preparatory work. Our work also included interesting and illustrative exchanges with the Soviets. One month before the preparatory meeting was to begin in Madrid, I met in Washington, D.C., with my Rumanian CSCE colleague and invited him and his delegation to lunch on the first day of my arrival in Madrid. He accepted, and after the meal, told me that he had mentioned this lunch to the Soviet ambassador, who had indicated interest in a similar session. My response, that I would be pleased to meet with the Soviet ambassador, came as something of a surprise to my colleague, since the United States had not been talking with the Soviets at a high level since the invasion of Afghanistan the previous December. But I could not conceive of being in a meeting with thirty-five states and not talking to one of the parties. (I had previously cleared this position with the Department of State, which had authorized me to use my own judgment on the matter.)

At any rate, the Rumanian delegate was pleased, and called me an hour or two later to tell me that Soviet Ambassador Yuri Dubynin was also pleased. [1] How should we meet? There followed one of those little dances that lend to negotiating with the Soviets a certain kind of frustrating charm. I suggested meeting over lunch the next day at a site of Dubynin's choice; he, after all, knew the good restaurants, while I had just arrived in an unfamiliar town. But my Rumanian interlocutor had to call back with the word that the Soviet insisted that I decide where we were to meet. It was clear that Dubynin wanted it to appear that I was the one requesting the meeting. So be it, I said; if that is what he wanted, we could lunch at my apartment.

Dubynin arrived the next day accompanied by his deputy, Sergei Kondrashev, a KGB general who remained the highly capable Soviet number-two man throughout the review conference. It was a long meeting. I began by telling them, in a moderate voice, that I was a firm anti-communist and believed that their system not only ran contrary to American values but posed a threat to the security of my country. On the other hand, I also wanted them to know I was very

1. Dubynin, the Soviet Bilateral Ambassador to Madrid, was an expert on CSCE matters, and I expected him to be my counterpart throughout the Madrid Review Conference. However, he was removed to a secondary position after the preparatory meeting.

serious about the CSCE meeting and believed we could achieve something constructive because it made no sense for us to do anything else. In retrospect, it was a crisp, but useful exchange.

Later that night, my Russian-speaking and experienced State Department deputy, Warren Zimmermann, informed me that Kondrashev had been in touch with him and wanted to meet again the next day. At first I hesitated, but then I asked Warren to tell Kondrashev that the Jewish high holidays began the next night, and I would be in the synagogue. I would, however, be happy to meet with the Soviets the following evening. We did. It was important to me to send the Soviets the message that I was open about my being Jewish.

Soviet intransigence can be turned to Western advantage, we learned during the preparatory process. After extensive preparatory consultations with our allies in the NATO caucus, our delegation had agreed simply to accept the agenda and modalities previously agreed upon in Belgrade, rather than take up precious time fighting to improve them. We wanted the agenda of the main Madrid meeting to begin with a taking of inventory as to how the Helsinki Final Act was being observed, so I suggested to the Soviets that both sides quickly agree to the Belgrade rules, rather than each of us trying to alter them in different directions. I mentioned that, while it was an election year in the United States and an agenda fight would be politically popular at home, we were prepared for a very short, pro forma preparatory session so that in November during the conference proper, we could get down to the serious, substantive issues that divided us. The Soviets shortly rejected this proposal, and the result was a nine-and-a-half week preparatory phase. In the end, they capitulated and gave us much more, in terms of the agenda, than we had gotten at Belgrade. Throughout this entire process, I kept the European allies fully informed of my bilateral discussions with the Soviet delegates; the result was a high degree of Western harmony. The NATO caucus meetings convened at least three times a week during the review conference, and sometimes as often as six times a day when events dictated such frequent consultation.

In Madrid, I had between 375 and 400 hours of private meetings with the Soviets outside of the formal sessions. Much of it was unproductive, particularly the discussions with the Soviet delegation chief, Deputy Foreign Minister Ilichev, an able, experienced, and committed communist "survivor." Ilichev seemed most at home with a brief calling for rigidity; that penchant, together with his extraordinary volubility, left little room for progress. But there were some productive exchanges, and simply engaging in dialogue was important to keep the lines open for the possibility of movement.

It is hard to provide profound generalizations from our Madrid negotiations. I did not view the conclusion of a written agreement as our most important objective at Madrid. While we would welcome an agreement that served our interests, we believed that there were other purposes to the Madrid meeting as well. My experience as a lawyer had taught me that a written agreement was not necessarily a sign of a successful negotiation; one can reach written agreements not in accord with one's primary objectives.

So, throughout the Madrid process, we tried to keep one supremely important fact in mind: that the agreement we signed at Helsinki in 1975, an agreement that defined important behavior patterns, had not been observed by the Soviet Union. I reminded the Soviets continually of their transgressions of the Helsinki Final Act. Nor did I become hesitant even as I got to know my Soviet counterparts better on a personal level. I consistently told the Soviets that our differences were fundamental, that a cosmetic agreement was unacceptable to the United States, and that therefore we were quite ready to agree to disagree. Although I did not intend such bluntness as a negotiating tool, it turned out, in retrospect, to have been a useful one.

Standing firm for the values that underlay the Helsinki Final Act, even if such firmness precluded a written agreement, was one major U.S. objective. Another was maintaining Western alliance cohesion. In fact, as the Madrid meeting unfolded, this objective grew in importance, and we worked hard to achieve it. I believe we did achieve it, on the whole, with great success. Frequent NATO caucus meetings were helpful; the allies knew that the United States would not take a position at the conference without first discussing it with them. Maintaining alliance, and more broadly, Western, cohesion had its tricky moments: There was the question of the non-NATO members of the European Community and their relationship to the Western caucus; there was the matter of the "neutrals" and the "non-aligned" (the CSCE process includes countries such as Malta, San Marino, Cyprus, and Yugoslavia); and there was our intention to use Madrid as a springboard for the integration of Spain into NATO.

Beyond their positive impacts on the Western alliance, our efforts to work toward alliance cohesion had a salutary effect on our negotiations with the Soviets. The Soviets once complained to me they were having to make all the concessions, while we were making virtually none. I explained that, while they came to the plenary sessions with heavily padded proposals, our Western proposals had already been modified and refined in intra-alliance negotiations. Our proposals had to meet the legitimate concerns not only of our allied, but of our various publics. So we came to the plenary sessions with honed-down, lean proposals that represented close to what we actually wanted, while the Soviets came with inflated proposals that naturally had to submit to the most drastic surgery. It became evident that Soviet intransigence, extremism, and even occasional boorishness in their negotiating behavior were actually contributing to Western alliance cohesion and in fact to a toughening of the Western delegations in defense of Final Act values. This alliance cohesion survived our disagreement over whether "business as usual" could be resumed after the imposition of martial law in Poland; the allies wanted to get back to serious negotiations, while the U.S. delegation thought "business as usual" to be an impossible concession to Soviet aggressiveness. The resolution of this issue is evidence of the value of pursuing the difficult, but rewarding, course of consultation and extensive discussion with allies.

What finally allowed a reasonably "successful" conclusion at Madrid? Several factors occur to me. First, we went to Madrid prepared. We had secured our base in our own government, with key domestic constituencies in the American public, and with our allies. Each of these constituencies proved crucial in maintaining a firm, consistent line at the review conference. Secondly, we held firmly to reasonable positions during the conference itself. There is an important difference, it seems to me, between firmness and rudeness; while the line may be hard to define, it surely exists and one recognizes it, even if only in the breach. Our entire effort at Madrid was on the side of firmness. We named names, we made disagreements clear, we upheld the key values that are the foundation of the Helsinki Final Act. But we did all of this without being rude or unnecessarily offensive. My own observation is that the Soviets, however occasionally discomfited by such firmness, in the long run were grudgingly grateful for it. They knew where they stood with us at all points. Such clarification of issues made the agreements we reached possible. In fact, were I to draw any one, general lesson from my experience of three years in Madrid, it would be that firmness and clarity of purpose are the prerequisites to any successful negotiation with the Soviet Union. Contrary to the widely circulated opinions of some Western accommodationists, such clarity and firmness, which they view as confrontational, serve to make agreement possible, not impossible.

11 PERSONAL EXPERIENCES IN COMMERCIAL NEGOTIATIONS

Robert D. Schmidt

I come to the subject of U.S.–Soviet negotiations with a different history than that of many seminar participants. My experience has been strictly in the commercial area, as Chairman of the Computer Business Equipment Manufacturer's Association and President of the American Committee on East–West Accord. Perhaps my perspective on other presentations at these seminars along with some anecdotes of my own will provide fresh insights into Soviet negotiating.

COMMENTS

Ambassador Paul Warnke proposed that, in arms negotiations, neither side needs a deal. In contrast, Benjamin Huberman argued that the domestic political situation in the United States sometimes does create a need for arms control negotiations. Without contesting this issue, let me say the Soviets do need a deal in commercial negotiations because they very much want to trade with the United States. Sometimes they desire such trade simply because of our reputation, not because they could really obtain a good deal. But Soviet economic development is so far behind ours that they feel a strong need to acquire certain advantages we have to offer as trade partners.

The Soviets take great pains to create reasons for having discussions, seminars, and the like. This is true in education, medicine, and almost every other field with which I have been involved. Their initiative in these and other areas sparked the growth of U.S.-Soviet trade.

I agree with Helmut Sonnenfeldt that economic sanctions have little effect on any Soviet action after the fact. Perhaps we could use the threat of economic sanctions effectively before the fact, particularly if we exploited the back channel and if our economic ties were strong enough. However, I believe it would be necessary to develop a heavy economic dependence upon each other for trade to have any significant effect on the overall conduct of Soviet foreign policy. Nowadays, the volume of trade is too small to provide significant leverage.

As Robert McClellan noted, U.S. businessmen have been allowed to travel freely in the Soviet Union. I may have visited more factories than any other American—at least that is what the Soviets tell me. In fact, I have visited some factories to which other people have been denied access. At times, U.S. embassy personnel have asked me to take them along on my visits. Unfortunately, that is not possible. The Soviets allow me to take some of my own people, but not officials. I once tried to arrange for several Department of Defense officials to visit a Soviet factory. The Soviets discussed the issue for six months before they finally refused.

McClellan discussed the issue of linkage, as did Helmut Sonnenfeldt. I do not think it is possible to obtain linkage between economic and political issues.[1] The Soviet system, more than any other system in the world, is extremely fragmented. The leaders of the various bureaucratic sectors are firmly entrenched and do not often interfere in one another's business. Within certain limits, Foreign Trade Minister Nikolai Patolichev can say to members of the Politburo or the Council of Ministers, "I don't want to let arms control interfere with our trade negotiations." But I think the opposite happens too—top officials in the Ministries of Foreign Affairs and Defense simply tell everybody else that arms control is none of their business. So the Soviets are fairly good at minding their own business. They learn that lesson at an early age.

---

1. One participant noted the possible inconsistency in the two ideas that, on the one hand, we could not obtain any benefits from linkage and political issues with the Soviets, while, on the other hand, they really want trade with us.

Several seminar participants corroborated my own experience in negotiating with the Soviets—that the negotiations require endurance. In his book, Hedrick Smith discussed the fishermen on the Amur River who were fishing through the ice.[2] One fisherman had accumulated a large pile of fish, while the rest had very few. Somebody asked this man to what did he attribute his great luck in catching all these fish. Through cold and stiffened lips he replied, "Luck had nothing to do with it, only endurance."

Speaking from their experiences in arms control negotiations, several seminar participants noted the Soviets' need for high-level approval, which can only be obtained by returning to Moscow. This is true in trade negotiations as well. The various Soviet ministries are organized alike: They all require the top officials in Moscow to approve many apparently trivial decisions of lower functionaries. Frequently, after a delegation returns to Moscow, minute decisions require interminable discussion within the ranks, especially in the case of a sizeable contract. The contract passes through several levels of the Ministry of Foreign Trade, into the Politburo, and then into the U.S.A. and Canada Institute.

One quirk of negotiating with the Soviets is that they never allowed us to remove clauses from a standard form contract. They have many kinds of standard form contracts. Clauses cannot be removed from such contracts, but one can add clauses that entirely obviate the clause that one wishes to remove. Apparently, the Soviet negotiators must have to answer too many questions if the clause is actually removed.

In business dealings with the Soviets, I, too, have often used a back channel, especially during negotiations with the Ministry of Culture about the Hermitage Exhibition (see below). If the Ministry of Culture would not give me what I wanted, I would go to Dzherman Gvishiani at the State Committee on Science and Technology or his predecessor. Sometimes I would also speak to Georgi Arbatov at the U.S.A. and Canada Institute. Usually, if I waited long enough for these back channels to operate, I would get what I wanted from the Ministry of Culture. The State Committee on Publishing was also involved in the Hermitage Exhibition because they were planning to publish several books with reproductions of the art pieces. The chairman of that particular committee is a real hard-liner with whom it is

2. Hedrick Smith, *The Russians* (New York: Ballantine, 1976).

extremely difficult to do business. So I utilized the back channel not only to bypass the Ministry of Culture but also to handle the State Committee on Publishing.

PERSONAL NEGOTIATING EXPERIENCES

My first dealings with the Soviets were in 1969, when my employer, Control Data Corporation, sold them a used computer for a nuclear installation at the Joint Institute for Nuclear Research (JINR) at Dubna. Dubna is an open, free installation; scientists from all over the world go there. This sale was encouraged by the U.S. Department of Energy, though they have subsequently renounced it for reasons of their own.

I spent a great deal of time putting together deals between the Soviet Union and Control Data, until 1982, after the Russians had moved into Afghanistan, when I was denied legal exemption from "freedom of legal seizure." The U.S. Congress is empowered through the U.S. Information Agency to give freedom from legal seizure to various art exhibitions in the United States. They can use this power to prevent the seizure of property that arrives with exhibitions from countries like Czechoslovakia and the Soviet Union by those with claims on property in these countries.

We were planning to bring a large, $115 million art exhibition from the Hermitage to the United States to exhibit in five different locations, starting in Washington in May 1980. In the fall of 1980, President Carter was fighting for his political life and was not particularly anxious to bring a Soviet exhibition of that size to Washington art museum. So we were denied the legal exemption to freedom of seizure. Consequently, the Soviets would not ship the exhibition. At that point, Control Data had invested $1.25 million in the project, most of which was irretrievable. It was impossible to sue the U.S. government, so we had to simply accept the loss.

Thus, Control Data is now waiting for settlement of arms control and other political issues before striking up more deals with the Soviets, because it is not possible to trade profitably with an adversary nation without some guarantee of long-term stability. Most programs in a company like Control Data require seven to ten operating years to pay back the initial start-up costs. So, for any program to succeed, there must be a solid basis upon which to operate. In 1972, when we became heavily involved in U.S.–Soviet trade, we believed there was a firm foundation for relations and did not foresee the adverse reaction of the late '70s and early '80s. Over the next eight years, as the political situation gradually worsened, the trade situation also deteriorated. Notably, this process has not changed the basic Soviet desire for trade.

The director of the Hermitage, who initiated the above-mentioned exhibition, uses a Control Data computer at the Academy of Sciences to catalogue the inventory of 3.5 million art objects stored in the Hermitage. Because of the size of the cataloguing project, he wanted his own computer to develop an archival retrieval system in conjunction with the Louvre and a museum in Italy. But he did not have the hard currency necessary to purchase the computer. Moreover, he could do little to obtain that currency, as the museum charges only a five kopek admission fee.

So he asked me to devise a plan that would allow him to earn some hard currency. (Incidentally, almost everyone wants hard currency in the Soviet Union, and the authorities do little to stop them.) This is how the idea for the exhibition originated. The museum was supposed to receive half of the proceeds from selling the reproductions of art objects that were manufactured for the exhibition. They projected earnings of $5–6 million over a period of three to three-and-a-half years. I inserted a clause in the contract stipulating that they must use these proceeds to buy a Control Data computer. They agreed because that was what they wanted in the first place. I had simply created a method for them to earn the payment for the computer.

When I was in Moscow in April 1984, I met with Deputy Minister of Foreign Trade Vladimir Sushkov, who is their chairman of the U.S.-U.S.S.R. Trade and Economic Council. Sushkov startled me by proposing to ask American companies to build computers with Soviet technology for shipment to the Soviet Union. He wanted to know whether the U.S. government would agree to such a proposal. I told him that several companies would probably be very interested in the proposal, but that the government would probably not grant its approval.

As an example, I cited a technology that Control Data bought from the Soviets to harden and coat tools. It is a titanium nitrite process that is performed in a vacuum. For some reason, U.S. engineers have never been able to solve the associated technical problems, but a professor in a Soviet institute did. His technology uses a coating, not a deposition, which hardens the tools and makes them last eight to ten times longer. The technology is seldom used in the Soviet Union because the only producer is this one professor at an obscure institute, and he lacks the facilities for large-scale production.

We are now beginning large-scale production in the United States through a joint venture that Control Data formed with some other companies. The joint venture company designed and manufactured some new coating machines possessing the industrial characteristics that one would expect from a piece of U.S. equipment. But when we tried to obtain a license to export our titanium nitrite coating machine to the Soviet Union, the U.S. government refused, despite the fact that we had initially acquired the technology from the Soviets. Apparently, the technology was on the government's list of sensitive items, and there was no way to circumvent that list.

I told Sushkov that story in answer to his question. Evidently, he understood, because he did not even mention his computer proposal when he was visiting the United States in May during the U.S.-U.S.S.R. Trade and Economic Council's meeting.

Academician Gurii Marchuk, now the Chairman of the State Committee on Science and Technology (GKNT), was once very interested in cooperating with Control Data on certain new architectures the Soviets had developed. His enthusiasm declined when the Soviets learned how to build a 25 million instruction-per-second array processor that is usually used for seismic oil exploration. Marchuk, who is not a computer expert, believes this is one of the world's fastest computers. He told me, shaking his finger, that GKNT would accept no more computer exchanges unless we give them one of ours in exchange for one of theirs. This was an absurd proposition because, even with that new special purpose computer, the difference between their level of sophistication and ours is a factor of almost ten. Their best machines can do 25 million instructions per second. By contrast, machines that perform roughly 1 billion instructions per second are not uncommon in this country.

Academician Dzherman Gvishiani, Deputy Chairman (GKNT), with whom I participated at the Institute of Applied Systems Analysis, could not resist using a little competitive blackmail. He informed me 250 chief executive officers from Japanese companies wanted to sell their technology and products to the Soviet Union. They all spent an entire week describing to the Soviets what they had for sale. Gvishiani told me this as a veiled threat: The Soviets had other potential suppliers if we would not give them what they wanted. Even so, he knows very well that our defense strategy precludes computer companies like Control Data from doing anything that would cause the Defense Department to lose sleep at night.

If one earns a measure of trust, the Soviets can become quite open. They will reveal things, do things, and say things that they would not have in the early days. The following anecdote about my attempt to create a Russian jade business illustrates this point. The Soviets were selling Russian jadite in 10- and 20-pound chunks. It was a version of the very light, apple-green Burmese jade of which the Chinese are so fond. We did not see very much of it, but we did once buy some 20 tons of raw jade, which we then had cut, polished, and set in jewelry in Hong Kong.

The Soviets wanted to form a joint venture to convert the jadite into jewelry so they could derive added value from the rocks. I liked the idea but said there were some things I would have to know before devising a business plan. I wanted to know where the jade came from, and I wanted some experts to examine the mines to determine whether this business would last for ten or fifteen years, or merely a few months. Initially, we were dealing with Raznoexport but then a different company, Almazjuvilerexport, assumed responsibility for the deal. These two companies made arrangements on four separate occasions for me to visit Lake Balkhash, the supposed mining site located near the Chinese border in a desolate part of the Soviet Union. One problem in arranging my visit was that they could find no place for me to stay other than in a tent, and they did not want to subject me to that.

Finally, the president of Almazjuvilerexport called me aside for a private conversation. He said, "I would dearly love to do that joint venture with you, but the reason you cannot get permission to visit the mine is that there is no mine. I have never been to the site, but I am sure that there is no mine. There is simply a place where people collect pieces of rock that are lying on the ground. Thus, it will be of little use to form a joint venture, because we cannot complete the job."

So, he advised me to "stop talking to them." Of course the "them" to which he referred were his own people, but he offered this advice because he wanted to preserve my good will for possible future ventures. Naturally, I heeded his advice. The point is that the Soviets can be quite honest and sincere about things, although not all of them are that way all of the time.

12 NEGOTIATING AND THE U.S. BUREAUCRACY

Herbert F. York

U.S.–Soviet negotiations are very complex because every negotiation actually involves several negotiations. This chapter will focus in particular on the bureaucratic negotiating process within the U.S. government, and how it influences negotiations with the Soviets. One simply cannot understand what the United States does, or even more importantly what the United States does not do, without understanding the bureaucratic processes that underlie those events and non-events.

In a bilateral negotiation, there are really three distinct negotiations. There is a negotiation among all the interested parties in Washington. There is probably something like that in Moscow, although it is a bit mysterious. And then, of course, there is a negotiation between the delegations of the two countries in Geneva.

In the case of the comprehensive test ban (CTB) negotiations, the situation was further complicated by the inclusion of the British. It was a trilateral negotiation. This added two more negotiations: a negotiation among the British in London, and a secondary negotiation between the United States and Britain in which we sought, not always successfully, to work out a common position to present to the Russians. The Russians always referred to the United States and Britain as one side, which of course we were. But that did not mean that our positions were always indentical, and therein lie some of the problems with multilateral negotiations.

THE ROLE OF THE BACKSTOPPING TEAM IN THE COMPREHENSIVE TEST BAN NEGOTIATIONS

The backstopping team is comprised of representatives of several agencies, each of which wishes to have some input into the process, and each of which has some expertise that might be needed or some viewpoint that should be heeded.[1] For CTB, the backstopping team included the usual agencies: the Department of Defense (DOD), the CIA, the Joint Chiefs of Staff (JCS), the Department of State, and the Arms Control and Disarmament Agency (ACDA). It also included the Department of Energy (DOE) because DOE, not DOD, is responsible for conducting nuclear weapons tests. Thus, the CTB negotiation, whose purpose was to stop nuclear testing, was supposed to stop a major activity of the Department of Energy.

In the CTB, and to some extent in the antisatellite (ASAT) negotiations, the situation was different from many other negotiations in one important respect. In the CTB case, there were certain agencies that were not interested in simply contesting or modifying certain details of a particular proposed test ban; they wanted no test ban at all. They flatly opposed the president's objectives. These agencies often couched their objections in terms of modifications to a specific proposal, but in reality they flatly opposed a test ban. The DOE opposed the test ban because it was their activity that was to be banned. The Joint Chiefs opposed a test ban because they genuinely felt, and were never convinced otherwise, that testing was essential to maintain the reliability of our nuclear stockpile. Thus, all other issues, such as verification, were really secondary. The agencies did not want a comprehensive test ban at all, and no simple modification could satisfy them.

1. There was considerable discussion of backstopping. One person asserted that the U.S. government needed to be better organized for negotiations and that National Security Council control of backstopping committees could assure this. A controversial suggestion to resolving interagency squabbling over negotiating positions was the appointment of a special high-level official to work full time to coordinate among the components of the backstopping effort. One speaker responded that one person doing this for each negotiation was too much and that perhaps the director of the Arms Control and Disarmament Agency could fulfill the coordinating role. Another participant said we needed more non-political expertise on the Soviet Union, which could be especially helpful in crises. Someone responded that this would be hard to develop because diplomats and others did not like long stays in Moscow and that anyway it would not guarantee a more rational view of the Soviet Union.

The case of the ASAT negotiations was similar, but less extreme. Within the DOD, the Air Force was interested in pursuing antisatellite negotiations. They had certain reservations about the idea, but nevertheless expressed interest. On the other hand, the Navy, or at least elements of it that entered the debate, was flatly opposed to a ban on antisatellite weapons. Regardless of what the Russians do, they argued, the United States must have antisatellite weapons in order to cope with Soviet sea surveillance systems. By a curious quirk, the representative of the Office of the Secretary of Defense (OSD) on the backstopping committee was an admiral who adhered to the Navy position. He worked for OSD, not the Navy, but he was the OSD representative on the backstopping committee and was personally opposed to a ban on ASATs.

As noted above, the backstopping committee for the CTB included representatives of the DOE and the JCS, agencies that flatly opposed any positive result. Furthermore, the individuals were in some cases even more strongly opposed than their agencies. That was significant because the process of formulating negotiating instructions is essentially bureaucratic. And in any bureaucratic process, the person who wants only to obstruct the process has an advantage. There is nothing one can do to satisfy him. He does not want some particular change. He simply wants no agreement at all. The natural advantage of a bureaucrat in that position is easy to exploit. One does not even have to be a particularly smart bureaucrat to exploit it, although a smart bureaucrat can do so more effectively.

There are two common tactics for exploiting this advantage. One is to propose that the problem of the moment is much more complicated than it appears and that it requires further study. The other is to insist that the problem is beyond our level of competence and must be resolved at a higher level. In the case of the CTB backstopping group, a higher level meant the cabinet-level committee, called the Special Coordination Committee during the Carter administration and the Committee of Principles during the Eisenhower administration. Even in good times, any question referred to the cabinet level would take weeks or months to resolve. And after the hostage crisis, Afghanistan, and the presidential primaries, the Special Coordination Committee never again resolved anything in regard to the CTB.

The following specific examples illustrate use of the first tactic: saying that a problem is too complicated and requires further study. The first example also illustrates the problems of three-party negotiations. About halfway through the CTB negotiation, each side had advanced major proposals concerning the placement of ten special seismic stations for monitoring compliance with a test ban on the territories of the other party. Then, all delegations returned to their capitals to work out details of the locations of these stations in the United States, Britain, and the Soviet Union.

The individual proposals were then jointly discussed at a cabinet meeting in London that happened to convene during a rare London snowstorm. The dustmen, who put sand on the roads to facilitate driving, were on strike. As a result, the meeting was late, it was short, and the main topic was how to clear the roads. There was little time to discuss a comprehensive test ban, but it was decided that the United Kingdom, because it is a small country, should have only one seismic station, unlike the United States and the Soviet Union, which would have ten each. This decision came as a surprise to everyone, and brought the negotiation to a standstill.

To move the process off dead center, I immediately proposed that Secretary of State Cyrus Vance meet with British Foreign Minister David Owen to work out a compromise somewhere between the British proposal of one station and the Soviet proposal of ten. Secretary Vance was just beginning preparations for that meeting when the delaying tactic was employed. The representative of the Joint Chiefs said that Vance should not independently discuss the question of seismic stations with Owen because it had important military implications that required further study. The tactic worked. The resulting study delayed a Vance–Owen meeting for several months.

The study finally concluded that in fact Vance should meet with Owen on this issue. But by the time that conclusion was reached, there had been an election in Britain. Prime Minister James Callaghan had been replaced by Margaret Thatcher, who considered the CTB a bad idea. She was willing to follow the American lead in pursuing a CTB. However, she felt that if one seismic station was enough for Callaghan, it was certainly enough for her. And so we were stuck. The two-month delay was totally effective; it removed the possibility of working out a more acceptable position.

Ironically, ACDA, which supported a test ban, also helped to slow things down in this case. A few purists in ACDA argued that we should not allow the British to settle for an intermediate position. They insisted that the British must accept ten seismic stations. If the British want to play in this league, they argued, they must play by the rules.

Thus, the ACDA purists also delayed the process by adhering to an extreme view on the other side.

A second example of bureaucratic-induced delay concerns one of the more bizarre situations I faced. In late 1978, we invited the Soviets to send a delegation to the United States to look at our proposed seismic stations, just to see what they were like. We hoped to allay Soviet fears by removing some of the mystery. As is usual with the Soviets, they took a long time to answer. However, more than six months after receiving our original invitation, they finally did agree to come. Eager to get the program ready, I immediately reported the Soviet acceptance to Washington.

Unfortunately, the DOE raised two issues. First, they asked who was going to pay for the visit. It was a matter of $25,000, essentially for hospitality. The norm in such exchanges is that the Soviets pay for us when we visit there, and we pay for them when they visit here. This $25,000 issue blocked progress for almost two months because the money did not appear anywhere in the budget. DOE representatives claimed that there could be trouble if the House Armed Services Committee learned that we were spending unbudgeted funds. The people who raised the issue were delighted that there were problems, but they adopted a pose of helpfulness. Nevertheless, they insisted that the issue be resolved before reconfirming the invitation and completing the plans for the visit.

The second issue DOE raised was that scientific exchanges with the Soviet Union must be based on agreements either between the two science academies or between various agencies in the government. In this case, they argued, there is no agreement to exchange data on seismology, and we must conclude such an agreement before the Soviets can visit our stations. This was an awkward situation indeed. We had already invited them. Six months later they had agreed to come. I had told them that we were eagerly awaiting their visit. Then I received instructions from Washington not to arrange anything. So I spent the next two months telling the Russians that there were some minor administrative questions to be settled. We finally did resolve these issues. It delayed their visit for over two months, but the Soviets did come.

A third example of delay concerns a proposal to put a seismic station in Obninsk, a city near Moscow that has a Soviet seismic observatory. Most U.S. officials thought it would be quite worthwhile to have an operating American station in the Soviet Union. It is difficult to find anything wrong with the idea. We could acquire a lot of information from such a station. Also, the Soviets would learn more about our equipment and possibly overcome some of their fears about placing American equipment on Soviet territory. In addition, we would get some seismic data from a site that was already thoroughly understood.

But when the full backstopping group considered the proposal, the group's negative members argued that we should not even propose putting a station in Obninsk without first developing a complete plan for its use. They raised the following questions: How will we get it there? Who will install it? What kind of data will we get back? What will we do with that data? We must study the problem more thoroughly, they argued. That tactic delayed our presentation of a proposal to the Soviets for more than three months.

We advanced the proposal on December 5, 1979, during the period between the capture of the U.S. Embassy in Tehran and the Soviet invasion of Afghanistan—a singularly difficult time. The proposal came just at the end of the round. The Soviets indicated that they were unsure about the proposal, but they would grant it "the consideration it merited," and would discuss it back in Moscow. Our next meeting was after the invasion of Afghanistan. We were instructed to proceed very slowly. Some of us understood that as an order to move faster because, by that time, we were not in fact moving at all. But we proceeded even more slowly.

As one reaction to the Afghanistan invasion, the president further restricted technology transfer. The seismic station is a technological device, a seismometer that, with the sole exception of one cryptologic device involving some modern technology, uses straightforward, simple technology. Moreover, the cryptologic device could have been omitted at the Obninsk site. There was no real technology transfer problem, but the same people tried to anchor their objections on the newly imposed policy. Now they argued that we thoroughly study every component of the device to determine whether it should be placed in the Soviet Union.

In sum, we had a great idea: to put a seismometer in the Soviet Union as part of an experiment before the final CTB treaty would be signed. It would have moved the process forward, and we would have obtained some data. But the idea was blocked by those who argued we should study the technology transfer implications of the issue. The bureaucratic delay was then transformed into a permanent roadblock by events in Afghanistan, Tehran, and the presidential primaries. The notion that a cabinet-level committee was needed to settle the issue brought the process to a complete stop, because it was not possible to convene a cabinet-level meeting on such a trivial issue under the prevailing circumstances.

I returned to the subsequent round of negotiations with a curious set of instructions. I was told not to mention the December 5 proposal unless the Soviets mentioned it first. Evidently, they had exactly the same instructions. We had struck an impasse. Thus, we ended the negotiations one year later without ever again mentioning our proposal, whose purpose was, in my judgment, entirely beneficial to the United States.[2]

THE EVOLUTION OF U.S. CTB POSITIONS

Strong opposition within the executive branch led to another peculiarity of the CTB negotiations. The path that the negotiations followed was entirely contrary to folklore about how arms control negotiations usually proceed. Specifically, the American position steadily hardened throughout the negotiation, while the Soviets made occasional concessions that lagged behind changes in the American position. This situation is contrary to the usual view that the Soviets stand firm while we gradually make concessions to them.

We began with the position that a CTB should be forever. It should, of course, allow for withdrawal, and it should allow for review, as do other arms control agreements. But our position was that the purpose was to permanently ban nuclear testing, assuming the necessary conditions were met. The Soviets, however, wanted only a temporary ban. They argued that the Chinese and French would eventually have to participate for the test ban to be a viable enterprise, and without Chinese and French participation, the Soviets were unwilling to permanently ban nuclear tests. The United States did not want a treaty that explicitly depended on what the French and Chinese might do. We wanted a permanent treaty that provided both sides the option to withdraw.

2. One participant suggested that the "nay-sayers" in the bureaucracy were strengthened in the latter part of the 1970s by a conservative shift in U.S. domestic politics. He said we needed better political timing in our negotiations to know how far we can go in our arms control positions. Others added that we needed strategies for accomplishing our arms control objectives while they are still relevant, noting the obsolescence of SALT II by the time it was finally signed.

Early in the Carter administration, it became evident that the opposition to a test ban was stronger than the president had anticipated. So he began indirect negotiations with those senators who were predisposed against ratification of a CTB. In particular, Carter sought the support of officers and officials who had influence with those senators. He also began to make compromises designed to keep the support of those who were wavering and to obtain the support of others who were opposed. In his first such concession, Carter agreed to scrap the idea of a permanent test ban in favor of a five-year ban.

Unfortunately, Carter ordered this switch in the U.S. position just after the Soviets had come around to agree to our initial proposal for a permanent test ban. But the Soviets again followed our lead and agreed to a five-year ban, whereupon the president made another concession. Under pressure from the DOE and the Defense Nuclear Agency, he decided that a three-year ban was the longest we could tolerate. The Soviets never agreed to three years, but they did agree to continue discussing other issues, while postponing the question of the duration of a test ban.

Another fundamental U.S. position going into the negotiations was that a nuclear test ban was a very simple thing. There were to be "no nuclear weapons tests," and no nuclear weapons tests meant *none*. After about one year, and under pressure from advocates of continued testing, the administration decided that it should formulate a more precise definition of a "nuclear test." It agreed that there are certain experiments that really are not nuclear tests, but that might look like nuclear tests, and that might be necessary and legitimate to conduct. These were called "permitted experiments." The U.S. negotiators formally introduced this idea of permitted experiments about one year into the negotiations, promising to present definitions of such activities shortly. In virtually every round, the Soviets would ask for our position on permitted experiments. But three years later, when the negotiations finally terminated in 1980, we still had not developed a definition. That particular point went unsettled.

The initial U.S. position on the potential manufacturers of the seismic stations also hardened as the negotiations continued. At first, the United States said that it did not matter who manufactured the stations. At one time, Ambassador Paul Warnke said they could be manufactured anywhere, perhaps in Japan, even in Mongolia. What matters, he argued, is that the stations meet certain technical performance criteria, and we should negotiate those criteria with great care. So we proceeded to negotiate the technical parameters describing these seismographs. We said that we knew how to make them, and we wanted the Soviets to see our equipment, but we did not care where the seismographs were made.

Then, after two years of negotiations, in another attempt to compromise with those opposed to a CTB, the president decided that the seismic stations to be placed in the Soviet Union must be manufactured in the United States. The Soviets never rejected this new proposal outright, but they never accepted it either. And in one rather heated exchange, the Soviet representative accused me of treating the Soviets as if they were a sixth-rate Arab nation, a puzzling but vivid analogy.

We changed our position on other issues too. At first, the U.S. said that it must receive data from seismic stations in the Soviet Union "in a timely fashion." Halfway through the negotiation, we decided that we must receive the data "in real time."

Also, we began with the notion that the preamble would present no problems. We have written numerous preambles in the past and, by referring to previous texts, we assumed it should be easy to elaborate a preamble for this treaty. Again, two years into the negotiation, the American position changed. The bureaucratic opponents of the CTB said that we had been promising too much in past preambles. We had been making "pie in the sky" promises we could not keep. Thus, it was concluded that the preamble should be negotiated with great care to avoid making excessive promises. Despite both British and Soviet proposals of various alternate preambles, we refused even to discuss the preamble after the first six months. Only during the last six months, when there was nothing else to do, did we resume preamble discussions.

With regard to the natural advantage of the "nay-sayers," there are only two possible solutions. First, if the president is interested enough to become personally and continuously involved, he can simply regularly overrule anyone who is trying to block any agreement at all. The other solution is to deny them coequal status after negotiations have begun. It is necessary, for political and other reasons, that all interested agencies be involved on a coequal basis in deciding whether there ought to be a negotiation. But once that is decided, it is self-defeating to grant coequal status to agencies and people whose sole real goal is to stop the negotiation or cause it to fail.

OTHER OBSERVATIONS

The chapter will conclude with several observations on negotiations in general. One has to do with the role of visitors. While I was negotiating the CTB, we had, among others, two Washington visitors — one from ACDA and one from the National Security Council staff. Each of them came to familiarize themselves with the process. Beyond that, they had no specific purpose. However, the Soviets were convinced that these visitors were special emissaries who came to float trial solutions to a particular issue on which we were deadlocked, and they so interpreted remarks that were made during informal, essentially social, visits.

In one particular case, the Soviets interpreted the visit as a signal that we were preparing to compromise on the issue of how many seismic stations to put in the United Kingdom. As a result, they made a minor, tactical concession. They agreed to talk about something that they had previously refused to discuss. So we discussed the issue and thanked them for their concession. They later said that they felt we had deliberately tricked them into making this concession by parading visitors to create the impression that we were ready to compromise.

That raises the issue of the Soviet approach to compromise. One could argue that the Soviets use rigidity and stubbornness as a tactic to elicit U.S. compromises. Be that as it may, their willingness to make concessions does not hinge only on our firmness. It also depends on their assessment of our seriousness about the negotiating process. In the Soviet viewpoint, the worst mistake that one of their negotiators can make is to offer a concession that is not reciprocated. Thus, if the Soviets decide that we are not serious, they will refuse to make real concessions on even the most trivial matters.

Midway through the test ban negotiation, the United States became unwilling to discuss issues that we previously wanted to discuss such as the preamble and permitted experiments. We steadfastly and continually refused to discuss those issues. Meanwhile, Leslie Gelb, shortly after he left the State Department, published an article in *Foreign Policy,* corroborated by other stories in the American press, saying that the CTB was going nowhere.[3] At that point, the Soviets became convinced there was no chance for a test ban negotiation to succeed, and from then on, they refused to make even the slightest concession.

3. Leslie H. Gelb, "A Glass Half Full...," *Foreign Policy* 36 (Fall 1979): 21–32.

13 THE ROLE OF CONGRESS IN U.S.–SOVIET NEGOTIATIONS

R. James Woolsey

The problem of negotiating with a totalitarian country on behalf of a democracy is an awesome one, especially when agreements have to be ratified by two-thirds of the voting members of the upper body of that democracy's legislature. It is fundamentally a difficult problem for us because of the U.S. Constitution. With its marvelous eighteenth-century balancing of interests, it has done a superb job of protecting our individual liberties. But the Constitution is not designed for efficiency. Deep frustrations over this particular issue, among others, have led such distinguished observers of the process as Lloyd Cutler to begin to think in terms of a parliamentary or a modified parliamentary system for the United States. So this is not a simple problem with simple remedies. It is embedded in what Madison and his colleagues did in the summer of 1787 in Philadelphia.

Second, the problem is worse when we have separate political parties controlling the executive and legislative branches. For much of the last thirty years, that has been the case. It may be even more of a problem in the future if political analyst Horace Busby's notion proves correct — that there is a Republican lock on the presidency and that there will be a continued predominance of Democrats in at least one, and perhaps both, houses of Congress for a number of years.

Third, this issue of U.S.–Soviet relations and arms control is not something that we can keep on the back burner. My own bias in negotiating with a stubborn, chess-playing adversary that takes the long view, such as the Soviet Union, is to do what Llewellyn Thompson did in the Austrian State Treaty negotiations. In that case, the United States had a sound position and stuck to it for years. Eventually, for their own reasons, after Stalin's death, the Soviets decided that all of these American positions—which they had said were totally non-negotiable for so long—*were* negotiable and that we could reach an agreement. But it is very difficult, verging on the impossible, to wait the other side out as Thompson did on subjects that are as central to our political process and to virtually every American's hopes and fears about the future as U.S.-Soviet relations and strategic weapons.

High emotions have, for some years, attended the issues of nuclear war and arms control. Arms control has been viewed by some people as the curse that will undo us and, by others, as the grail that will save us. These different attitudes have produced, at least over the course of the last five or six years, a very high degree of politicizing of the arms control process. This began most recently with President Jimmy Carter's rejection of the 1974 Vladivostok accords and his adoption of a new proposal in March 1977—one that was immediately pulled off the table after it was rejected by the Soviets when yet another proposal was substituted for it. The politicizing of arms control continued all the way through the congressional arguments about SALT II—arguments at least partly responsible for the treaty's withdrawal from the ratification process after the invasion of Afghanistan—and through the nuclear freeze campaign. Over the course of the last two administrations, until relatively recently, political figures of both parties have come into office in the executive branch with the idea that much of what went before should be scrapped and that whatever their administration does has to be brand new so they can win the appropriate credit.[1]

This phenomenon was not peculiar to President Reagan in 1981, nor is it the whole story of what happened even early in Reagan's administration in the area of arms control. It has happened in both Democratic and Republican administrations. It has led, particularly in these times of single interest constituencies and political action com-

---

1. Several participants agreed with this assessment. Some went on to argue that an important obstacle to a bipartisan approach to arms control is the tendency for much of the public discussion to be stated in hyperbolic terms. They suggested that the rhetoric of political leaders on nuclear issues be toned down in order to help reduce unrealistic public expectations of arms control.

mittees (PACs), to a situation in which groups on both sides of the debate have found it convenient, desirable, and in some cases even necessary to use U.S.–Soviet relations and arms control as devices to build up their lists for direct mail campaigns or raise funds for their PACs. Even groups that were previously oriented toward procedural reform in the U.S. government, such as Common Cause, have found it desirable to shift focus and to enter the substantive debates on specific weapon systems and specific arms control proposals.

The politicizing of arms control has also led Congress, at least some parts of it, to toy with the idea of what are, in effect, indirect negotiations with the Soviets—as in the cases of the "quick freeze" and various proposals for legislative moratoria, in which the executive branch is essentially treated as a casual bystander to the process. In short, the interaction between our political and constitutional systems, the strong hopes and fears associated with arms control with the Soviet Union, and the current American political structure—including powerful single interest constituencies and PACs—has nearly created a political irony: Republicans can get most anything ratified that they can negotiate, but have a hard time negotiating anything, while Democrats might be able to negotiate something, but cannot get it ratified.

There have been times, however, when relations between the executive branch and Congress have stimulated a greater ability to negotiate successful arms control agreements with the Soviet Union. Doubtless, both of the efforts in the following examples were aided and assisted by many back channel contacts between the executive branch and Congress. One was in 1963, during the period when the United States and the Soviet Union were going back and forth about the number of verification sites that would be necessary in order to have a CTB, and the negotiations, at least at that time, appeared to be stalemated. The Dodd–Humphrey Resolution recommending an atmospheric test ban only, which had broad support in the Senate, played a very important part in the process that led to the negotiation of such a ban. It signaled that, from the point of view of a very broad cross section of Congress, an atmospheric test ban was a reasonable deal that could be ratified. I think the resolution thereby probably improved the prospects of that agreement being negotiated with the Soviets.

A similar, though less clearcut development occurred in the 1960s concerning the Joint Atomic Energy Committee's long-term opposition to the Multilateral Force (MLF) for NATO defense. It was, of course, the MLF that was one of the main barriers to the Nuclear Non-Proliferation Treaty (NPT). Once opinion in favor of the NPT crystallized within the executive branch and the Joint Atomic Energy Committee, there was a give-and-take between Congress and the executive branch on that issue, and it became clear that it was possible to drop the MLF and move toward the NPT. Thus Congress can, by signaling a somewhat unlikely and unaccustomed similarity of views between the executive branch and an important part of the legislative, be a help rather than a hindrance to arms control. The outside world knows that we have an eighteenth-century constitution that sets us at odds with one another much of the time, and when we show that we are not at odds, we tend to look — as well as be — unified. So the executive–congressional split is an opportunity to be exploited in the name of showing national unity, as well as a continuing problem. [2]

Regardless of what administration is in power, how might one deal with Congress on arms control in order to accentuate the positive and somewhat suppress the negative? First, we must agree not to try to bypass Congress. Not only is that illegal in the area of arms control under the 1961 Arms Control and Disarmament Act, which requires that obligations to limit U.S. armaments be approved by treaty or by statute, but it is politically foolish. Some observers, during the 1984 election campaign, suggested that if there is a change of administration, and the new one still could not get two-thirds of the Senate to approve an arms control treaty, then we should do something with an executive agreement. I believe that that way lies madness. Even if there were some way to do it legally, it simply joins together the substantive and the procedural opponents of the administration's course of action and ensures a long, bloody, and bitter fight over any arms control agreement.

I do think there are some institutional and substantive steps that might make it easier to deal with the relationship between the executive branch and Congress on arms control issues. First, it has long been a question whether members of Congress ought to be on delega-

2. One participant suggested a "sense of the Senate" resolution that would outline general criteria for an agreement before the United States entered into arms control negotiations. He said that this resolution would have to strike a balance by being specific enough to be meaningful but general enough to provide negotiating flexibility. Mr. Woolsey agreed in principle that there could be a time for such a step, but cautioned against tying the negotiators' hands.

tions or not. Certainly, President Woodrow Wilson is widely regarded as having made a terrible blunder by assigning no Republicans to the Versailles negotiations after World War I. President Warren Harding corrected that in 1921–1922 when he put a number of Senators on the delegation to the Naval Armaments Conference.

It is harder now. In the Carter administration, members of Congress were permitted to sit in on negotiations. But in these days of easy travel, many may do so, causing a great deal of confusion. The position has been reversed by the Reagan administration, although members of Congress who go to the site of the talks have been able to meet with the Soviets in sessions outside the formal negotiations. From the point of view of propriety, the second procedure is better than the first. But a congressional role might better be assured if a representative two or four members (just notionally, a liberal Democrat, a liberal Republican, a conservative Democrat, and a conservative Republican) were given some special status on major negotiations and the ability to participate in the negotiations themselves. Members of Congress are far more willing to pull together as a team when they are dealing with the Soviets than when they are back in the halls of Congress. Administrations might consider trying to move together with the leadership in the House and the Senate toward some special status for a *very* limited number of members of Congress in future arms negotiations. This would mean moving essentially as Harding did rather than as Wilson did.

Second, it is important to try to keep the substance of arms control agreements relatively simple and to have them operate in terms of incentives. In general terms, the build-down approach that the Reagan administration presented in October 1983 has those features. That is, it attempts to discourage certain types of weapon systems, rather than to ban them or to engage in detailed mutual force planning with the Soviet Union. Whenever one gets involved in such mutual force planning—which is, in a sense, what the SALT I interim accord on offensive systems and SALT II did—one ends up with agreements that look like they were drafted by a group of lawyers, which they usually are. Then they resemble nothing quite so much, as Gerard Smith once said, as some of the materials from his law school course on future interests. If you have not studied future interests in law school, let me tell you that is no compliment.[3]

---

3. One participant made a similar point, asserting that a preoccupation with details had led American arms control policymakers to overlook broader issues. He suggested that we need a

By aiming for agreements that operate in terms of incentives rather than prohibitions or detailed force planning, it is reasonable to try also to temper somewhat the objectives for strategic arms control between the United States and the Soviet Union. Such an attitude toward objectives would make arms control agreements with the Soviets carry a bit less freight than if they are regarded as final agreements for all time — agreements destined either to save the world or destroy it. Instead, arms control agreements might come to be thought of as arrangements that tend to put some English on the ball, to put the tiller over a few degrees — arrangements that incline the programs of both countries in a somewhat different direction or channel modernization rather than attempt to stop it or engage in detailed force planning on a system-by-system basis. The tone and attitude that accompany a relatively simple agreement that tries to operate in terms of incentives, such as the build-down does, would also have the indirect effect of lowering the temperature of the argument between the executive branch and Congress and between the political parties.

Finally, since it is election season, I will speculate about one type of gimmick to illustrate my point — a gimmick not necessarily applicable to the current situation but one that makes my point about bipartisanship. One feature of the politicizing of U.S.-Soviet relations and summitry over the course of the last decade or so — a game at which, by the way, I consider Richard Nixon a past master and Jimmy Carter both less skillful and less lucky — has been that administrations want to scrap everything that went before to prove that their proposal is fresh and that they ought to get all the credit for anything positive that happens. In some cases there might be utility in trying to break out of that mold in a procedural and symbolic way. I have no particular enthusiasm for summits; I have always liked Dean Acheson's statement that at a summit, if the president fumbles the ball, there is nobody between him and the goal line. But I do think there may be some utility in having relatively regular meetings between American and Soviet leaders, perhaps not annually, but rather every two or three years. These meetings might have a very general, simplified agenda of the sort that President Reagan described as reasonable in a press conference in July 1984.

more comprehensive framework that encompasses the forces of the two sides as a whole. Another pointed out that verification requirements might conflict with the desire for simple agreements. Mr. Woolsey replied that the verification requirements of the incentives approach might not have to be as detailed as those needed for limits on specific weapons.

I wonder what the impact would be on the highly politicized nature of U.S.-Soviet relations in American politics if the two presidential candidates would agree before the election that both would be inclined, sometime during the six months following the election, to have a summit with the Soviet leader, and that both would attend regardless of who won the election. Certainly, whoever won would head the U.S. undertaking, would have the most prominent role, and would conduct private discussions at some point with the Soviet leader. A president within his first six months in office, whether newly elected or reelected, is in a honeymoon period and has very little to fear politically from a person he has just defeated. That might incline both parties, whoever won, to have not only the defeated presidential candidate of the other party, but probably a few congressional leaders from the other party on the summit delegation as well.

In terms of ceremony, and to some extent in substance, this idea would require leaders of both parties and Congress and their two parties to cooperate. I do think the phenomenon of members of Congress who tear into one another on the floor of the Senate and then show up in Moscow on a delegation and stand side-by-side in arguing with the Soviets might well prevail in the world of summitry as well. It might also indirectly help lower some of the expectations, hopes, and fears that both sides might have about using or suffering from various turns that U.S.-Soviet relations might take just before an election. After the election, the American people would see two people who are the leaders of their parties, and who have just been in a very hard-fought campaign against one another, stand side-by-side dealing with the Soviet Union. This approach could induce political changes in what is often a very poisonous political attitude on these issues. I firmly believe the most partisan political advisers to both presidential candidates would normally strongly oppose this sort of thing, and therefore I think it is probably worth talking about.[4]

4. This idea elicited interest and several comments. One participant argued that no newly elected president would share power with his defeated adversary. He added that the same objective might be accomplished by sending two powerful senators from the party opposite that of the president. Another questioned the value of sending the defeated candidate, since he would have no power and would be a mere symbol.

14 HOW THEORY MIGHT HELP

Roger Fisher

Can theory help us learn from experience, both for arms control negotiations and for U.S.–Soviet negotiations in general? Any lesson learned about negotiation is a generalization that applied from one circumstance to another. Generalizations imply a theoretical framework. We all have some concepts about negotiation in mind. If we learn from last year and apply those lessons to next year, we are using theory. The better our theory, the more we should be able to learn.

Recently at Harvard, we had two Soviet teachers of negotiation visiting us from the Moscow State Institute for International Relations. We have been developing a common set of concept and designing a pilot course that we and others might co-teach to mid-career diplomats. We repeatedly ask ourselves what we would teach people about how to negotiate better. It is a good question: What ideas will help us improve the process — not simply describe what happens, but help improve both theory and practice?

Our basic question is: What is the best advice that we could give to two negotiators who were negotiating with each other? And then: In what way would that advice be different if we were coaching only one side? Rather than start with an adversarial assumption, we ask what is the best way to dance if we are going to be dancing together? If

I were negotiating with Ed Rowny, what would be the best advice people might give us jointly on how to negotiate? [1]

Applying theory to practice. Figure 1 illustrates the situation. You practitioners are in the real world in the lower half of the figure, while we academics are in the upper half—the world of theory. Each world can be divided into what is (left), and what might be (right). Now in the real world when a message or cable comes in (in the lower left quadrant), you have a real situation—a problem. In the lower right quadrant, there are specific ideas about what might be done—ideas about specific actions that might be taken in the real world. Safe at Harvard, we academics describe (in the upper left quadrant) in generalizations and abstractions what is going on and (in the upper right quadrant) prescribe what in a general way is needed—for example, "more understanding." We tend to go back and forth on this academic level. It does not provide much help to a negotiator. We make the sort of generalized remarks that I am making now; remarks that may be absolutely true, but nonetheless seem worthless to anyone who has to deal with specific facts in the real world.

Some social scientists, wanting to bridge the gap between practice and theory, study problems and come up with descriptions in great detail. They will, for example, count the cables coming out of the State Department and conclusively prove that more cables are sent out on Friday afternoon than any other day of the week, or something else that may be equally true and equally useless.

What we need to do is to bring theory to bear on practice. This means (I) identify the problem clearly; (II) diagnose it in terms of cause and effect—what is creating this problem? If that is the diagnosis, then (III) what is our prescription in general terms? Finally (IV), we apply that prescription to a particular case.

I. WHAT IS THE PROBLEM?

The purpose of a negotiation is to get results—a good outcome. We are more likely to do something well if we know what we are trying to do. If we hope to have successful negotiation, it will help if we are

1. There was considerable discussion of the question of the importance of technique. Several participants offered the view that technique in negotiations was less important than other factors such as political will and the calculation of one's interests. One said that in some

Figure 1.   Bridging the Gap between Theory and Practice.

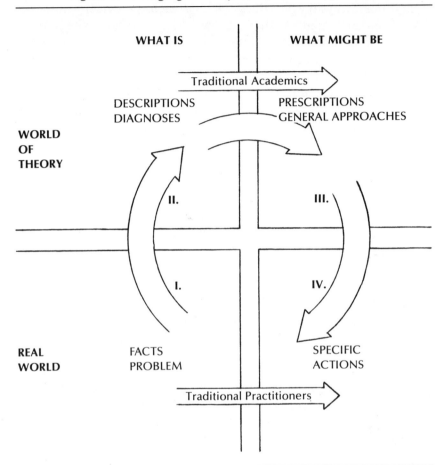

able to define success. Just what do we mean by "a good outcome?" It turns out to involve seven distinct elements.

1. *Better than any ALTERNATIVE.* The first thing that we would ask of any negotiated outcome is that it be better than what we could do for ourselves without having to negotiate. We are looking for an

negotiations no agreement was possible, regardless of technique. Professor Fisher agreed that technique may look like only a small factor compared with historical, political, and economic constraints, but said it constitutes 100% of what a negotiator can change. Another participant added that good technique could get a negotiator somewhat more than he might otherwise get; and that bad technique could ruin a whole negotiation.

outcome that is better than the available self-help alternatives. Agreement is not always the best thing. Do not reach agreement just for the sake of an agreement. It ought to be better than your alternatives. Part of preparing for a negotiation is to think about one's Best Alternative To a Negotiated Agreement (BATNA). It provides a base against which to compare any proposed agreement. We give students an exercise in which it is impossible for them both to reach agreement and to serve their best interests. Yet students frequently go right ahead and agree anyway, despite a preferable alternative.

2. *INTERESTS are satisfied.* The second thing to look for in a negotiated outcome is whether or not it satisfies interests. My interests should be well satisfied, yours should be acceptably satisfied, and community interests tolerably satisfied. The party with whom I am negotiating should be sufficiently satisfied to say "yes," and community interests sufficiently met for it to tolerate our agreement. A successful outcome needs to have something in it for all parties involved. This means that it is important for me to understand with great clarity exactly what your interests are so they can be sufficiently met to make an agreement of benefit to you.

3. *A good OPTION.* We would like a substantively efficient solution to the problem. We would like it to be the best, or nearly the best, of the options upon which we might agree. I want you to have enough—just enough—for you to be satisfied and then, consistent with that, for my interests to be accommodated optimally. If you do not care about an item, I would like to pick up the slack. We want to achieve an elegant solution to the problem, with no waste. It should be so well crafted that it cannot be made better for me without becoming worse for you, nor better for you without becoming worse for me.

4. *High LEGITIMACY as measured by objective criteria.* No one wants to be "taken." Each of us cares about legitimacy. It turns out that most parties involved in a negotiation care more about not being "had" than they do about the precise figures or numbers in an agreement. We want the outcome to be legitimate as measured by law, precedent, equal treatment, reciprocity, or some other such principle. It should be legitimate as measured by objective standards, not just one side telling the other it is all right. Each side wants to be able to justify its decision by reference to some objective criterion.

5. *Wise COMMITMENTS.* At the end of the negotiation, we want a deal. We want commitments made as to who is going to do what and

who will refrain from doing what. The substantive content of these commitments is what the negotiation is presumably about. The commitments should be realistic, easy to implement, "compliance prone," and no more extensive than needed to serve the interests involved.

6. *Effective COMMUNICATION.* A good outcome is one that is reached efficiently, with no wasted effort. We do not want to spend six years doing what could be accomplished in six weeks. Efficiency requires good communication. If we are sending smoke signals in a high wind, or not listening, or talking primarily to the audience, or sending mixed messages, it is hard to reach agreement — particularly within a short time.

7. *Good RELATIONSHIP.* Finally, we would like this transaction to be concluded in a way that will make the next transaction easy to negotiate wisely, efficiently, and amicably. We do not want to reach an agreement here in such a way that it is the last time the other side will trust us. We do not want to leave a bomb under their chair so that after they have signed an agreement the whole thing blows up. One feature of a good outcome is that we leave this negotiation with a good working relationship.

That is the way I would define a good outcome. In theoretical terms, this is what we mean when we say that we want to have successful negotiations. The trouble is that quite often in negotiations — including negotiations between the United States and the Soviet Union — we fall short of the ideal. This gap, between what we would like to have happen and what actually happens, is our "Problem" down there in the real world, in the lower left quadrant.

II. DIAGNOSES: POSSIBLE CAUSES OF A POOR OUTCOME

Of the many explanations of less-than-optimal outcomes, let me suggest a few by looking at two common styles of negotiations: "soft" and "hard," "dove" and "hawk." On the question of alternatives to a negotiated agreement, a soft negotiator will say, "We've got to talk; we have just got to meet with the Soviets." The hard negotiator says, "The Soviets walked out. We do not have to negotiate. It's their fault." These two different styles reveal implicit assumptions about the negotiation process, assumptions that touch all seven of the identified elements.

A soft negotiator insists on a friendly relationship. Who cares about the merits as long as we have good relations? A hard negotiator wants to win on the substance and often ignores the relationship. A soft negotiator will insist on agreement. A hard negotiator will insist on his or her position. (Both are likely to pay too little attention to their underlying interests.) A soft negotiator, assuming that one has to make concessions, will concede generously. A hard negotiator, making the same assumption, will concede stubbornly. A soft negotiator talks about what he or she will do and makes offers. A hard negotiator talks about what he or she will not do and makes threats.

An example of a negotiation between two soft negotiators occurs when I negotiate with my wife. I come home from the office and say, "I know you would like to go to the movies." She says, "I know you would rather go out to a restaurant for dinner." We quickly agree to go first to dinner and then to a movie. We come home late, broke and exhausted, only to discover that both of us would have preferred to stay home. This is a typical, sloppy, soft negotiation. It is not too damaging to the relationship but otherwise is hardly successful.

However, the main problem with being a soft negotiator occurs when I negotiate with someone who is hard. If I insist on negotiating and you say you do not have to, I have to buy you into the talks. If I insist on a relationship and you insist on winning, you say, "Fine, we will have a good relationship as long as I win." If I insist on agreement and you insist on your position, I end up agreeing with your position. And if I concede generously and you stubbornly, guess who makes all the concessions?

A hard strategy dominates a soft one — but not for long, because hard bargaining is contagious. Essentially, we and the Soviets have both adopted a hard strategy. We both insist on winning. Neither insists on serious talks. The Soviets have now walked out, and we have announced that we will not change our position.

What is wrong with what we are doing? The basic difficulty is that both soft and hard negotiators are making some common mistakes. One says we have to talk, one says we do not. Each ignores the alternatives away from the table. Whether or not you want to negotiate in a given case depends entirely on how well you can do through self-help away from the table. If you cannot do very well away from the table, then you talk. Both the Soviet Union and the United States have tended to ignore what they can do by themselves to improve their security. They have tended to focus their attention on how badly they can hurt the other side, not on their own BATNA.

Both hawks and doves tend to treat the relationship and the substance of a negotiation as trade-offs: *Either* we pay attention to the relationship *or* we work on the substance. During the period of detente, doves tended to say that peace with the Soviet Union was so important that we should not talk about our serious differences. Hawks tended to say that our differences were so important that we should not talk with the Soviet Union. Both, in my judgment, were wrong.

In a negotiation, it is not a question of being concerned either with the relationship or with the substance. Both are important. Each requires attention. A negotiator should pursue both concurrently but separately, on a two-track approach. Relationship issues are those of perception, understanding, emotion, trust, and communication. Substantive issues are those of terms, dates, specifications, and numbers — the kind of issues that will be incorporated in an agreement. The better a working relationship, the easier it will be to achieve a wise agreement on substantive issues.

Negotiators, however, frequently get relationship issues entangled with substantive ones. They try to use one set of issues as leverage on the other. One classic mistake is to try to convert a bad relationship into a good one by making substantive concessions. But rewarding bad behavior with a substantive concession is likely to lead simply to more bad behavior. It is equally unwise to damage a relationship because of substantive disagreement. The more serious the disagreement, the more important it is to maintain a good working relationship that makes it possible to handle that disagreement wisely. Limiting comunication makes effective problem-solving more difficult. Both the United States and the Soviet Union have fallen into that trap.

A soft negotiator insists on agreement — insists on reaching a joint position. A hard negotiator insists on his or her position. Both are making the same mistake of focusing attention on positions rather than on the underlying interests. The basic task is not to quarrel about positions that might please one side or the other, but to identify the interests — that is the concerns, needs, hopes, wants, and fears — of both parties.

Both hawks and doves talk about "concessions" and the need to be either stubborn or generous. But the concept of a "concession" confuses the process of generating options with the process of deciding among them. Judgment inhibits creativity. If there is no brainstorming free from commitment, we are unlikely to devise an optimal solution. The idea-generating process needs to be freed from the process of making commitments. We need to have more "walks in the woods" where possibilities can be jointly explored. We need to authorize members of a U.S. negotiating team to meet with members of a Soviet team under circumstances where it is clearly understood that wild ideas are to be freely considered and that nothing said constitutes a commitment of any kind. To negotiate only by concession, whether concessions be made stubbornly or generously, is almost certain to preclude the kind of inventing needed to produce a wise agreement.[2]

Whenever we begin a negotiation by announcing what we will or will not do, we are making a commitment. We are stating at the outset the answer to a problem that we have not yet heard. We are, in effect, telling those on the other side that their perceptions, their views, their ideas do not matter. "Please listen to us seriously, but we have already made up our minds." If we want the Soviets to be open to persuasion, it helps if we remain open to persuasion. If we want them to talk seriously, we need to be in a frame of mind that will take account of what they say. Commitments are things to be made at the end of a negotiation, not the beginning.

These, then, are some of the reasons why we do not reach good negotiation outcomes:

- We often ignore the real alternatives away from the table (underestimating some things we might do, not worrying enough about others);
- We focus on positions instead of interests;
- We fail to do enough inventing of options;
- We underestimate the importance of legitimacy;
- We let communication break down;
- We make commitments too early; and
- We fail to negotiate a good working relationship.

2. Several participants made similar points. One said that we should avoid thinking of negotiations as a process of making concessions; instead, we should think of them as solving problems in a continuing process, a "ripening process" that develops "terms of trade" for the negotiations. Others suggested exploratory talks enabling the two sides to sound each other out before committing to a position. This might obviate the need for major fallback positions.

The seven elements of a negotiation serve as a useful checklist to analyze any situation. If a negotiation is going poorly, what may be an explanation? Do I understand the other side's interests? Have we worked hard enough at inventing? Have communications broken down? Have I been sufficiently concerned with finding a result that will be legitimate in their eyes? And so forth.

III. PRESCRIPTIONS: WHAT ARE SOME GENERAL RULES OF THUMB?

Alternatives. As far as alternatives are concerned, you ought to know your best alternative to a negotiated agreement — your BATNA. This is not the worst you can do to the other side, but rather the best that you can do for yourself without their participation. What is the best that we can do for our security without an agreement with the Soviet Union? The best bargaining chips are those things that we want to do anyway. An MX missile intended only to scare the Soviet Union and not in our interest to deploy is not a BATNA. We do not want to find ourselves doing things we wish we had not done. Before going into a negotiation, we want to study our self-help alternatives and develop the one that is apparently best. In any negotiation, we want to be able to walk out knowing exactly where we are going and just what we are going to do. If we know our BATNA, every negotiation will be a success in the sense that we will not accept an agreement unless it is better than the best we could have done on our own. It may not be quite the best that we might have obtained, but it will be better than anything we could have done for ourselves.

Interests. In the area of interests, it is important to understand the other side. There is a risk that in studying the concerns of an adversary, we look at them from the outside. A scientist who studies insects under a microscope is likely to know everything about a beetle — except what it feels like to be a beetle. An adversarial negotiator is likely to make a similar mistake. A skilled negotiator is in tune with the other side's concerns. I tell students that they are not ready to negotiate until they can put the other side's case more persuasively than the other side can — and have an answer to it. Then they are ready to talk.

Put yourself in the shoes of those with whom you are negotiating. If you were in their place, what would you be caring about? Being respected? Being accepted as an equal? Being listened to? Looking successful? Often such intangible interests are far more important than numbers.

Options. In order to reach agreement on an excellent option, we should first invent many options and then decide among them. This means brainstorming without commitment, initially among those on our side and then with members of the other side. We need to learn how to take walks in the woods, how to get ideas on the table. I once told Paul Nitze that if he had asked my advice, I would have offered two suggestions on how to take a walk in the woods with less risk of appearing committed. First, always be talking about at least two ideas, not one. If there are two different options being discussed, it reduces the risk of conveying the impression that either one is an official position. Second, have such discussions conducted by a deputy or by someone else who is not the representative with full authority. Such practices help generate options free from commitment. There are many ideas — like the partial test ban — that are best invented and discussed before any government official becomes committed.

Legitimacy. Search for criteria that will both serve your interests and appeal to those on the other side as objectively fair. An agreement is more likely to be acceptable if it really is fair. At a minimum, it should look fair to the other side and their constituents. You should constantly be looking for standards of legitimacy that meet that test. Can we find a precedent in Communist Party doctrine? What did the last Party Congress say on the subject? How can we reconcile what we would like with what will strike them as legitimate?

A rough standard for an opening proposal is not to advance any suggestion that is more extreme than one you would advance to an impartial arbitrator. It need not be a middle position. It need not be the one that you think a judge would accept. But to maintain your credibility, it should not be a proposal more one-sided in your favor than you would advance to an impartial third party. If it is more extreme than that, it is likely to strike the other side as ridiculous, and undercut your ability to persuade. One guideline for a negotiator on how far legitimacy should temper his partisanship is to speak as though talking to an arbitrator; listen as though you were one.

Communication. Communication ought to be more prominent than it usually is in our consideration of how to negotiate. We communicate at many levels and in many ways — through personal contact, listening, non-verbal signals, empathy, understanding. A skilled negotiator absorbs information and transmits it accurately and effectively. Much communication takes place in informal settings, far removed from any negotiating table.

Relationship. In international negotiations, there is always another day. There is no such thing as the one-shot transaction. A diplomat is always negotiating a working relationship.

It is striking the extent to which international relations are discussed as though they were a phenomenon like the weather — something that is beyond our control and just happens. U.S.–Soviet relations are now described as bad or "cold." They used to be good. There is remarkably little discussion of the dimensions of a relationship — of the key elements by which one measures how good or bad a given relationship has become.

In January 1984, President Reagan gave a worldwide television address calling for a better working relationship with the Soviet Union.[3] Yet if his objective was really to improve the relationship, the president might have been far more effective if he had picked up the telephone, invited Soviet Ambassador Anatoliy Dobrynin over to the White House, and asked his advice about what to say or do that might improve the relationship. Asking advice is one of the best ways to build a relationship.

If there is one rule of thumb about building and maintaining a relationship it is this: Always consult before deciding on matters of mutual concern. A practice of consulting demonstrates that I have not yet decided; I treat your opinions as worth listening to; your concerns are of some importance; I am open to being persuaded; we are in touch with each other; I am talking with you, not about you to others. Other qualities of a good relationship are honesty, keeping commitments, being available, and keeping confidences.

Commitments. Finally, commitments. There are several kinds of commitments. An offer is a positive commitment. Essentially, an offer says, "Knowing what I know now, I am prepared to do this. Maybe you can talk me into offering more later, but at least now, this is what I am prepared to do." An offer can be specific without limiting future flexibility.

Negative commitments tend to limit flexibility. There are two kinds of negative commitments: The first is a "lock-in" — an assertion that I am unwilling to change my mind. "There is nothing you could say

---

3. See *The New York Times,* January 17, 1984, pp. 1, 8.

that would cause me to change my position." In a negotiation conducted by haggling, there is often an implied negative commitment: Each offer carries with it an implied statement that this is (perhaps) my last and best offer. Each successive offer undercuts that implied lock-in, tending to damage the credibility of any future statement that an offer is in fact the last offer. Even when it is, the statement risks being disbelieved.

The second kind of negative commitment is a threat of conduct that would be bad for both: "If you don't agree with my view on how to divide the rations, I will sink the boat." This is the negotiating game of "chicken." People are sometimes influenced by threats, but chicken is a dangerous game to play. It tends to reward players who are deceptive, extreme, and willing to take high risks. The threats involved in this style of negotiation tend to cut off communication, destroy legitimacy, damage a relationship, and preclude the development of an elegant solution that meets the interests of both sides. Threats, if made at all, should presumably be made only at the end of a negotiation, after all else has been tried.

IV. SPECIFIC ACTIONS: APPLYING THE THEORY TO A PARTICULAR CASE

Finally, theory should help us decide just what to do in a particular negotiating situation. One of the virtues of organizing our thinking about negotiation in terms of the seven elements that I have been discussing is that those elements serve as useful categories in all four quadrants of the Circle Chart illustrated in Figure 1—they help us understand the problem (the gap between present reality and a good outcome); they serve as a diagnostic check list to help us understand why things may be going poorly; they suggest some basic rules of thumb; and finally, they help us bring theory to bear on specific facts.

Some theoretical propositions may be perfectly true, such as a statement that "good negotiation depends upon experience, judgment, and timing," but not particularly useful. What are we supposed to do now? On the other hand, the proposition that it is desirable to invent multiple options before deciding among them has immediate relevance in a particular case. For example, the Soviets are opposed to the United States Strategic Defense Initiative or "Star Wars" program for research and development of defenses against missiles.

Before trying to decide what to do, let's privately invent a number of specific options that might draw verifiable and practical lines between permitted research on the one hand and prohibited development, testing, and deployment on the other. After we have generated a number of such options, we might discuss them with the Soviet delegation — all before making any commitment. In the same way, each element can be used to point us in the direction of specific actions we might want to take in a specific case.

The elements are also useful as categories into which to sort the otherwise chaotic array of specific do's and don't's of negotiation. Tips (such as "wear a clean shirt," "smile," "be on time") become more memorable and comprehensible if thought of as helping build a relationship by showing respect, openness, and reliability.

PUTTING IT ALL TOGETHER: NEGOTIATING POWER

In a given situation, my negotiation power — my ability to persuade you — will depend not only upon the skill with which I am able to handle each of these elements. It will also depend upon the orchestrated combination of them all. Again, the seven elements can serve as a checklist: Is each element in harmony with the others? For example, does an offer have legitimacy in the other side's eyes? Does it meet their interests? Could it be improved for them without hurting us? Has it been communicated effectively? Is it better for them than their walk-away alternative? Better for us? Would it be better for the relationship if we discussed the offer with them before making it? And so forth. Finally, our negotiating partners have their perceptions and their habits of mind. In the short term, the transaction costs of negotiating in a new way may exceed the benefits.

The seven elements provide a skeleton, a neutral theoretical framework.[4] Some such theory, I believe, can help anyone — Soviet or American, divorce mediator or diplomat, hawk or dove — sort out experiences and learn from them.

---

4. James Goodby commented that the Fisher model was too neat because of the presence of numerous parties on both sides, especially the U.S. side, where top leaders, executive agencies, Congress, and the press are all involved. Professor Fisher responded that the more complex a negotiation, the more useful he found it to have a handful of basic concepts.

15 CHAIRMAN'S CONCLUSIONS

Leon Sloss

The main importance of the lessons one draws from the negotiating history is that they will define, to a considerable extent, one's view of the role of arms control in our overall relationship with the Soviet Union. The following are my own conclusions about the negotiating process and how we might improve it.

We are entering a new era in negotiations with the Soviet Union. Particularly in strategic forces, whatever margin of military superiority the United States once enjoyed is now gone. A new generation of leadership is emerging in both countries. Public attitudes toward nuclear arms are changing in the United States and Europe. New technologies seem likely to change the role of nuclear and nonnuclear forces as well as the relationship between offensive and defensive forces. All of these factors will have an impact on U.S.–Soviet relations.

While some observers question the desirability of nearly continuous U.S.–Soviet negotiation, it appears likely that public opinion and allied relations will require just that. We will be involved in negotiations with the Soviet Union for the foreseeable future, and these negotiations will play a significant role in U.S. security policy. Thus, the United States should approach the process systematically and professionally, with a long-term plan—not in the haphazard way that has often been the case in the past. The first step is to be clear what negotiations are about, what we can expect to achieve, and what we should not expect arms control to accomplish.

The United States and the Soviet Union are engaged in a long-term competitive relationship. This is not likely to change soon. The competition for power and influence between the two superpowers takes place on a global scale and in many arenas in addition to the military balance. Arms negotiations are part of that competition. We negotiate about weaponry because we are competitors. Both sides use negotiations for a variety of purposes; reaching agreement is but one of them. Negotiations are used as a means of communications, for propaganda, to influence third parties, and, at least for the United States, to serve domestic political and alliance management purposes as well.

At the same time, the United States and the Soviet Union negotiate because they do have some common or congruent interests. Unless both sides saw benefits in negotiations, talks would not take place. Both sides have an interest in avoiding nuclear war and in curbing the proliferation of nuclear weapons. However, the common interests should not be exaggerated. Both states also rely on nuclear weapons for deterrence, for defense, and for political influence. So while both have been prepared to discuss limits on arms, they have also been reluctant to accept limits that they felt impinged on their security interests or appeared to be inequitable. Both have used negotiations as a means of curbing the arms programs of the other side while attempting to retain as much freedom as possible for themselves. Because both sides are suspicious of each other and because the two cultures are very different, arriving at common ground is difficult. But history shows it is not impossible.

Based on past experience, what should we expect from arms control negotiations? As Jonathan Dean put it in one of our seminars, "We can expect to achieve limited agreements with a rough balance of concessions on both sides." We should not expect negotiations to produce major reductions in arms, major reductions in defense spending, or a significant restructuring of the forces on either side in the near-term. We can look to arms control negotiations to provide an additional channel of communications between two hostile and suspicious states — an important aspect of their bilateral relations. Even when negotiations do not have specific results, they can reduce uncertainties and ambiguities and perhaps augment our mutual understanding of each other's military programs and strategic thinking. This could help reduce the prospect of overreaction to each side's actions that fuels arms competition and could be particularly dangerous in a crisis. Over the *very* long-run, negotiations may become part of a process that seeks to erode Soviet secrecy, isolation, and hostility and enhances dialogue and mutual confidence.

On the other hand, negotiations can also become an excuse for delaying needed U.S. defense programs. The prospect that agreement is "just over the horizon" or the belief that restraint will improve the climate for negotiation has been used as an excuse to defer funding of some necessary programs such as MX. The Soviets have been known to prolong negotiations in order to manipulate these political pressures in the West.

In assessing the role of negotiations in our overall security posture we need to keep the above points in mind. In particular, we should not expect too much from negotiations, and we should not always expect or even seek formal agreement. We must be aware that the Soviets do not always seek agreement either. Moreover, we can achieve some of our negotiating objectives (e.g., improving communications or reducing uncertainties) without signing an agreement. In this sense, negotiations with the Soviets differ from domestic negotiations.

IMPROVING U.S. NEGOTIATING TECHNIQUES AND SKILLS

Technique will seldom be the key factor in reaching agreement. There must be a willingness on the part of both sides to reach agreement and sufficient common ground to provide a basis for compromise. However, if the other factors exist, the way in which we negotiate can influence whether we arrive at agreement without undue delay, how we arrive at it, and whether the agreement is a good one, that is, whether it serves U.S. security interests.

There is much that we can learn about negotiating with the Soviets from past experience. Often U.S. negotiators have been poorly prepared to enter negotiations, knowing little about how the Soviets negotiate or about negotiating techniques that have worked in the past. The U.S. system affords less continuity in policymakers, negotiating teams, and backstoppers than does the Soviets'. We need to compensate for this. Detailed knowledge of past negotiations is the first requirement. Beyond this there are several ways in which we can improve.

First, a greater effort should be made to achieve continuity, at least among senior staff members, in our delegations and backstopping teams. Some changes in senior negotiators and staffs will inevitably occur with changes in U.S. political leadership. Nevertheless, too many personnel changes are made on political and ideological grounds at the expense of continuity—and often competence.

Second, all personnel involved in negotiating with the Soviets should receive formal training in such negotiations. Where possible, negotiating teams should train as a unit, using simulation techniques to test approaches and hone their skills. The Foreign Service Institute now offers courses in negotiations. These should be mandatory for *all* personnel involved in negotiations with the Soviets, and the courses could be strengthened and expanded to include training specifically addressed to U.S.–Soviet negotiations. Such courses should not only cover negotiating theory, but should also incorporate a good deal of practical advice from experienced negotiators.

Third, consideration should be given to the systematic use of simulation, or gaming, as a technique for training negotiators and negotiating teams. Simulation could be a useful way of testing negotiating approaches and also of exercising team dynamics.

Finally, we need to expand our understanding of the Soviet negotiating process and particularly of how the Soviets make decisions about arms control issues. This may never be entirely clear, given the secrecy of the Soviet system, but we should seek to improve our understanding as best we can. Specifically, U.S. officials need to be able to assess when it may be useful to make concessions in negotiations and when it is not, as that relates to the Soviet decisionmaking process.

THE NEED FOR CONTINUITY OF POLICY

A major point made throughout the seminars was the need for more continuity in U.S. arms control policy. Negotiations have been affected by changes in U.S. positions, often reflecting political shifts in the United States. To some extent this is unalterable. Incoming administrations are always likely to review policies toward the Soviet Union and arms control. It is inevitable that a new administration should introduce new key personnel. But radical breaks in policy and negotiating tactics disrupt the negotiating process. For example, in the past eight years we have seen two such shifts in U.S. negotiating positions on strategic arms. One came in March 1977 at the beginning of the Carter administration, when a new strategic arms proposal was advanced by Secretary Vance and Ambassador Warnke in Moscow. This would have altered fundamentally the agreement reached by President Ford and Secretary General Brezhnev at Vladivostok. At the outset of the Reagan administration there was a move to adopt different tactics and, subsequently, substantially revised arms control proposals with an emphasis on major reductions. Both initial U.S. proposals were later modified to make them "more negotiable."

In both cases the new directions had considerable merit on substantive grounds. However, these frequent shifts also reflect a lack of consensus in the United States on how to deal with the Soviets. Changes in negotiating tactics and positions are often an effort to "put a new face" on policy for political purposes. In fact, we have relatively little latitude over how we negotiate with the Soviets and what is susceptible to agreement. If we are going to negotiate at all — and I believe negotiation with the Soviets is inevitable — U.S. interests would be better served if we could arrive at a broad bipartisan consensus on a long-range strategy for these negotiations. Such a strategy should recognize the reality of the adversarial relationship on the one hand and the strong public demand for continuing negotiations on the other. We cannot expect to resolve fundamental differences or radically alter forces through negotiations but, at the same time, we cannot avoid an effort to work on those issues that may be negotiable.

A bipartisan consensus on negotiating with the Soviets will not be easy to achieve. Yet the importance of trying to achieve such a consensus seems obvious. The Soviets use arms control proposals and negotiations to manipulate and play on divisions of opinion in the West. To the extent that they can succeed in this effort, the Soviets will be less willing to negotiate seriously. If they see the U.S. government faced with pressures for unilateral arms reductions or with legislative injunctions to negotiate, their willingness to negotiate reductions is bound to recede.

How to achieve a better consensus? There is no magic formula. One suggestion would be to create a high-level, bipartisan advisory committee to advise the president on negotiating with the Soviets, to include members of Congress from both parties. This committee would develop negotiating proposals for consideration by the executive branch and review negotiating objectives and strategies. The President's General Advisory Committee on Arms Control and Disarmament (GAC) was formed to play such a role. Over the years it has become a more partisan body, reflecting, in general, the arms control philosophy of the prevailing administration. To perform the role envisioned here, it would have to be taken out of politics. This could be accomplished by extending the members' terms beyond one administation and by providing for appointments by both the executive and the congressional leadership.

This is but one suggestion. There may be other approaches that would work as well or better. The point is to recognize that arms control negotiations are part of a broader relationship. We need to develop a long-term view of how we deal with the Soviet Union that can win broad political and public support and that will sustain greater continuity of policy, tactics, and personnel. Without such a perspective, negotiating strategies and tactics will continue to fluctuate to the disadvantage of the United States and its allies.

APPENDIX

The following individuals took part in one or more of the three Roosevelt Center seminars entitled "Lessons Learned in Negotiating with the Soviet Union" and held in the spring and summer of 1984. The chapters in this book were presented and discussed at these seminars.

William Bader	SRI International
William Beecher	The Boston Globe
Robert Buchheim	Former U.S. Commissioner of the SALT Standing Consultative Commission
Ashton Carter	The Center for Science and International Affairs, Harvard University
Scott Davis	Roosevelt Center for American Policy Studies
Jonathan Dean	Union of Concerned Scientists
Robert Einhorn	Council on Foreign Relations
R. Lucas Fischer	Arms Control and Disarmament Agency
Roger Fisher	Program on Negotiations, Harvard Law School
Raymond Garthoff	The Brookings Institution
Sidney Graybeal	Center for Strategic Policy, Systems Planning Corporation

James Goodby	Ambassador and Chief of U.S. Delegation to the Conference on Confidence and Security Building Measures and Disarmament in Europe
Stephen Hadley	Shea & Gardner
Warren Heckrotte	Lawrence Livermore National Laboratory
Michael Higgins	Roosevelt Center for American Policy Studies
Benjamin Huberman	The Consultants International Group
Frank Jenkins	Science Applications International Corporation
U. Alexis Johnson	Former U.S. Ambassador to SALT
Max Kampelman	Head of U.S. Delegation and the U.S. Negotiator on Space and Defensive Arms
Helene Keyssar	University of California, San Diego
William Kincade	Arms Control Association
Jan Lodal	INFOCEL
Christopher Makins	Roosevelt Center for American Policy Studies
John Marks	Search for Common Ground
Robert McLellan	FMC Corporation
Dean Millot	The RAND Corporation
Fenner Milton	Roosevelt Center for American Policy Studies
Roger Molander	Roosevelt Center for American Policy Studies
Joseph Nye	Harvard University
Sol Polansky	Department of State
Edward Rowny	Special Advisor to the President and Secretary of State for Arms Control Matters
Ruth M. Schimel	Foreign Service Officer
Robert Schmidt	Jacobs Wind Electric Co.
Alan Sherr	Lawyers Alliance for Nuclear Arms Control
Walter Slocombe	Caplin and Drysdale
David Sloss	Arms Control and Disarmament Agency

Leon Sloss	Leon Sloss Associates, Inc.
Helmut Sonnenfeldt	The Brookings Institution
Howard Stoertz	Defense Consultant
Walter Stoessel	Former Deputy Secretary of State
Strobe Talbott	Time, Inc.
James Timbie	Office of the Deputy Secretary of State
Paul Warnke	Clifford and Warnke
James Wertsch	Northwestern University
Joseph Whelan	Congressional Research Service, Library of Congress
James Woolsey	Shea and Gardner
Herbert York	University of California, San Diego
William Zartman	School for Advanced International Studies

BIBLIOGRAPHY

STRATEGIC ARMS CONTROL NEGOTIATIONS

Bertram, Christoph. "SALT II and the Dynamics of Arms Control." *International Affairs,* October 1979.

Cutler, Lloyd N. and Roger C. Molander. "Is there Life After Death for SALT?" *International Security,* Fall 1981.

Garthoff, Raymond L. "Negotiating SALT." *The Wilson Quarterly,* Autumn 1977.

Hyland, William. "Commentary: SALT and Soviet–American Relations." *International Security,* Fall 1978.

Johnson, U. Alexis and McAllister, Jef O. *The Right Hand of Power.* Englewood Cliffs, N.J.: Prentice-Hall, 1984.

Kohler, Foy D. *SALT II: How Not to Negotiate With the Russians.* Coral Gables, Fla.: Monographs in International Affairs. Advanced International Studies Institute in association with the University of Miami, 1979.

Lodal, Jan M. "Finishing START." *Foreign Policy,* Fall 1982.

Makins, Christopher J. "The Superpower's Dilemma: Negotiating in the Nuclear Age." *Survival,* July/August 1985.

Muravchik, Joshua. "Expectations of SALT I: Lessons for SALT III." *World Affairs,* Winter 1980–1981.

Newhouse, John. *Cold Dawn: the Story of SALT.* New York: Holt, Rinehart and Winston, 1973.

Nitze, Paul H. "Living with the Soviets," *Foreign Affairs,* Winter 1984–1985.

Rostow, Eugene V. "Where are We Going in the Nuclear Arms Talks?" *Atlantic Community Quarterly,* Winter 1982–1983.

Smith, Gerard C. "SALT after Vladivostok." *Journal of International Affairs,* Spring 1975.

———. *Doubletalk: The Story of SALT I.* Garden City, N.Y.: Doubleday, 1980.

Talbott, Strobe. *Endgame: The Inside Story of SALT II.* New York: Harper and Row, 1979.

———. "Buildup and Breakdown." *Foreign Affairs, America and the World, 1983.* Vol. 62, no. 3, 1984.

———. *Deadly Gambits: The Reagan Administration and the Stalemate in Nuclear Arms Control.* New York: Knopf, 1984.

OTHER ARMS CONTROL NEGOTIATIONS

Bertram, Christoph. *Mutual Force Reductions in Europe: The Political Aspects.* Adelphi Papers #84. London: International Institute for Strategic Studies, 1972.

Dean, Arthur H. *Test Ban and Disarmament: The Path of Negotiation.* Published for the Council on Foreign Relations. New York: Harper and Row, 1966.

Dean, Jonathan. "MBFR: From Apathy to Accord." *International Security,* Spring 1983.

Hopmann, P. Terrence. "Bargaining in Arms Control Negotiations: The Seabeds Denuclearization Treaty." *International Organization,* Summer 1974.

Hopmann, P. Terrence and Timothy King. "Interactions and Perceptions in the Test Ban Negotiations." *International Studies Quarterly,* March 1976.

Keliher, John G. *The Negotiations on Mutual and Balanced Force Reductions: The Search for Arms Control in Central Europe.* New York: Pergamon, 1980.

Lall, Arthur S. *Negotiating Disarmament: The Eighteen Nation Disarmament Conference — The First Two Years, 1962–64.* Ithaca, N.Y.: Cornell University Press, 1964.

Terchek, Ronald J. *The Making of the Test Ban Treaty.* The Hague: Martinus Nijhoff, 1970.

U.S. Arms Control and Disarmament Agency. *International Negotiations on Ending Nuclear Weapon Tests.* Washington, D.C.: U.S. Government Printing Office, 1962.

U.S. Arms Control and Disarmament Agency. *International Negotiations on the Seabed Arms Control Treaty.* Washington, D.C.: U.S. Government Printing Office, 1973.

U.S. Arms Control and Disarmament Agency. *International Negotiations on the Treaty on Non-Proliferation of Nuclear Weapons.* Washington, D.C.: U.S. Government Printing Office, 1969.

U.S. Arms Control and Disarmament Agency. Office of Public Affairs. *International Negotiations on the Biological Weapons and Toxin Convention,* by Robert W. Lambert and Jean E. Mayer. Washington, D.C.: U.S. Government Printing Office, 1975.

U.S. Congress. House. Committee on Foreign Affairs. Subcommittee on International Security and Scientific Affairs. *East–West Troop Reductions in Europe: Is Agreement Possible?* Committee Report. Washington, D.C.: U.S. Government Printing Office, 1983.

ARMS CONTROL – GENERAL

Blechman, Barry M. and Janne E. Nolan. "Reorganizing for More Effective Arms Negotiations." *Foreign Affairs,* Summer 1983.

———. "Do Negotiated Arms Limitations Have a Future?" *Foreign Affairs,* Fall 1980.

Burt, Richard. "The Relevance of Arms Control in the 1980s." *Daedalus,* Winter 1981.

Dupuy, Trevor Nevitt and Gay M. Hammerman, eds. *A Documentary History of Arms Control and Disarmament.* New York: T.N. Dupuy Associates, 1973.

Kincade, William H. and Jeffrey D. Porro, eds. *Negotiating Security: An Arms Control Reader.* Washington, D.C.: Carnegie Endowment for International Peace, 1979.

Kofoed-Hansen, Otto. *The Negotiators: The Challenge of the Atomic Age.* Copenhagen: Munksgaard, 1964.

Luck, Edward C., ed. *Arms Control: The Multilateral Alternative.* New York: New York University Press, 1983.

Nye, Joseph S., ed. *The Making of America's Soviet Policy.* New Haven: Yale University Press, 1984.

Platt, Alan. *The U.S. Senate and Strategic Arms Policy: 1969–1977.* Boulder, Colo.: Westview Press, 1978.

Stanford Arms Control Group. Barton, John H. and Lawrence D. Weiler, eds. *International Arms Control: Issues and Agreements.* Stanford, Calif.: Stanford University Press, 1976.

U.S. Arms Control and Disarmament Agency. *Arms Control and Disarmament Agreements, 1980: Texts and Histories of Negotiations.* Washington, D.C.: U.S. Government Printing Office, 1980.

U.S. Congress. Senate. Armed Services Committee. *Arms Control Policy, Planning and Negotiating.* Hearings. 97th Cong., 1st sess., 1982.

Weiler, Lawrence. *The Arms Race, Secret Negotiations and the Congress.* Muscatine, Iowa: The Stanley Foundation, 1976.

York, Herbert F. "Bilateral Negotiations and the Arms Race." *Scientific American,* October 1983.

THE SOVIET APPROACH TO NEGOTIATIONS

Campbell, John C. "Negotiations with the Soviets: Some Lessons of the War Period." *Foreign Affairs,* January 1956.

Craig, Gordon. "Techniques of Negotiation." In *Russian Foreign Policy, Essays in Historical Perspective.* Edited by Ivo J. Lederer. New Haven, Conn.: Yale University Press, 1962.

Dallin, Alexander. *The Soviet Union and Disarmament: An Appraisal of Soviet Attitudes and Intentions.* New York: Praeger, 1964.

Dean, Jonathan. "Negotiating by Increment." *Foreign Service Journal,* Summer 1983.

Deane, John R. *The Strange Alliance: The Story of Our Efforts at Wartime Cooperation with Russia.* New York: Viking Press, 1946.

Dennett, Raymond and Joseph E. Johnson, eds. *Negotiating With the Russians.* Boston: World Peace Foundation, 1951.

Fischer, George, ed. *The Soviet Union, Arms Control and Disarmament: Background Materials on Soviet Attitudes.* New York: Columbia University School of International Affairs, 1965.

Garthoff, Raymond L. "Negotiating With the Russians: Some Lessons from SALT." *International Security,* Spring 1977.

Glagolev, Igor S. "The Soviet Decisionmaking Process in Arms Control Negotiations." *Orbis,* Winter 1978.

Holloway, David. *The Soviet Approach to MBFR.* Edinburgh: University of Edinburgh, Department of Politics, 1973.

Iklé, Fred. "On Negotiating With Communist Powers." *Foreign Service Journal,* April 1971.

Jonsson, Christer. *Soviet Bargaining Behavior: The Nuclear Test Ban Case.* New York: Columbia University Press, 1979.

Kertesz, Stephen D. "American and Soviet Negotiating Behavior." In *Diplomacy in a Changing World.* Edited by South Bend, Ind.: University of Notre Dame Press, 1959.

Luce, Claire Boothe. "How to Deal With the Russians: The Basics of Negotiation." *Air Force Magazine,* April 1979.

Payne, Samuel B., Jr. *The Soviet Union and SALT.* Cambridge, Mass.: MIT Press, 1980.

Scheidig, Robert E., Major. "A Comparison of Communist Negotiating Methods." *Military Review,* December 1974.

"Soviet Strategy and Tactics in Economic and Commercial Negotiations with the United States," National Foreign Assessment Center, Central Intelligence Agency, June 1979.

Wedge, Bryant M. and Cyril Muromcew. *Soviet Negotiating Behavior at the Geneva Disarmament Conference.* Princeton, N.J.: Institute for the Study of National Behavior, 1963.

Whelan, Joseph G. *Soviet Diplomacy and Negotiating Behavior: The Emerging New Context for U.S. Diplomacy.* Boulder, Colo.: Westview Press, 1983.

THEORY OF NEGOTIATION

Bartos, Otomar J. *Process and Outcome of Negotiations.* New York: Columbia University Press, 1974.

Beckmann, Neal W. *Negotiations: Principles and Techniques.* Lexington, Mass.: Lexington Books, 1977.

Druck, Daniel and Robert Mahoney. "Processes and Consequences of International Negotiations." *Journal of Social Issues,* Winter 1977.

Fisher, Roger D. *Basic Negotiating Strategy: International Conflict for Beginners.* London: Allen Lane, 1971.

Fisher, Roger and William Ury. *Getting to Yes: Negotiating Agreement Without Giving In.* Boston: Houghton Mifflin, 1981.

Iklé, Fred Charles. *How Nations Negotiate.* New York: Harper and Row, 1964.

Ilich, John. *The Art and Skill of Successful Negotiation.* Englewood Cliffs, N.J.: Prentice Hall, 1973.

Karrass, Chester Louis. *Give and Take: The Complete Guide to Negotiating Strategies and Tactics.* New York: Crowell, 1974.

Lall, Arthur, *Modern International Negotiation: Principles and Practice.* New York: Columbia University Press, 1966.

Nierenberg, Gerard I. *The Art of Negotiating.* New York: Pocket Books, 1984.

———. *Fundamentals of Negotiating.* New York: Hawthorn Books, 1973.

Raiffa, Howard. *The Art and Science of Negotiation.* Cambridge, Mass.: Harvard University Press, 1982.

Schelling, Thomas C. *The Strategy of Conflict.* Cambridge, Mass.: Harvard University Press, 1960.

Winham, Gilbert R. "Negotiation As a Management Process." *World Politics,* October 1977.

Winham, Gilbert R. and H. Eugene Bovis. "Agreement and Breakdown in Negotiation: Report on a State Department Training Simulation." *Journal of Peace Research* 15 (1978).

U.S. Congress. Senate. Committee on Government Operations. Subcommittee on National Security and International Operations. *International Negotiations.* Washington, D.C.: U.S. Government Printing Office, 1969-72.

Zartman, I. William, ed. "Negotiation." *The Journal of Conflict Resolution,* December 1977.

Zartman, I. William, ed. *The Negotiation Process: Theories and Applications.* Beverly Hills, Calif.: Sage Publications, 1978.

Zartman, I. William and Maureen R. Berman. *The Practical Negotiator.* Yale University Press, 1982.

INDEX

ABOUT THE EDITORS

Leon Sloss received his A.B. from Stanford University and his M.P.A. from the Woodrow Wilson School of Princeton University. He has served as Director of International Security Policy and then Assistant Director in the Bureau of Politico/Military Affairs, Department of State. In 1976–77, he was Assistant Director (and later, Acting Director) of the Arms Control and Disarmament Agency (ACDA). Mr. Sloss also served as head of the U.S. delegation to the Seabed Treaty Arms Control Review Conference in Geneva. After working as Vice President of SRI International and directing a special study of nuclear targeting policy for the Secretary of Defense, he started his own consulting firm in 1981, Leon Sloss Associates, Inc., which does studies of defense policy and arms control issues.

M. Scott Davis received his B.A. from the University of North Carolina and his M.A. in international relations from The Fletcher School of Law and Diplomacy. In 1980, Mr. Davis served as assistant to the Future Arms Control Panel at the Carnegie Endowment for International Peace. After working as a researcher at the Woodrow Wilson International Center for Scholars in 1981, he was an analyst on international security at Science Applications, Inc. in 1981–84. In 1984, Mr. Davis assumed his current position as Senior Associate at the Roosevelt Center for American Policy Studies.

ABOUT THE CONTRIBUTORS

Jonathan Dean is a graduate of the National War College and holder of a Ph.D. in Political Science from George Washington University. He has been dealing with East–West security issues for most of his professional career. In the 1950s, he served in Bonn as liaison officer between the U.S. High Commission and the newly formed Federal German government, including the Defense Ministry. In 1968–72, as Political Counselor at the American Embassy in Bonn, Ambassador Dean participated in the negotiations leading to the Four Power Agreement in Berlin. In 1973–78, he was the Deputy U.S. Representative to the NATO–Warsaw Pact Force Reduction Negotiations (MBFR) in Vienna, and in 1978–81 was the U.S. Representative to the talks. In 1981–84, Ambassador Dean was a Resident Associate at the Carnegie Endowment for International Peace. In 1984, he took his current position as Arms Control Advisor to the Union of Concerned Scientists.

Roger Fisher received his A.B. and LL.B. from Harvard University. He worked for the Economic Cooperation Administration in Paris in 1948–49 before beginning the practice of law with the Washington firm of Covington & Burling, working primarily on international law for foreign governments from 1950–56. In 1956–58, Professor Fisher served as Assistant to the Solicitor General, before going to Harvard

Law School as a Lecturer and then Professor of Law. In 1963–68 and 1979–80, he was a consultant to the Assistant Secretary of Defense for International Security Affairs. He is the author of the 1981 book *Getting to Yes: Negotiating Agreement Without Giving In* and is presently Williston Professor of Law and Director of the Harvard Negotiation Project at the Harvard Law School.

Raymond L. Garthoff graduated from the Woodrow Wilson School of Princeton University (A.B.) and received a doctorate in Russian studies from Yale University. After working for The RAND Corporation for seven years, he became an Estimates Officer at the CIA. In 1961–1968, Ambassador Garthoff served as Special Assistant for Soviet Bloc Politico/Military Affairs in the Department of State and later as NATO counselor for Political/Military Affairs in Brussels. His later positions include: Deputy Director, Bureau of Politico/Military Affairs in the Department of State; Executive Officer and Senior Advisor, U.S. SALT Delegation; and U.S. Ambassador to Bulgaria. In 1980, Ambassador Garthoff assumed his current position as Senior Fellow at the Brookings Institution. He is the author of the 1985 book *Detente and Confrontation: American–Soviet Relations from Nixon to Reagan.*

Sidney N. Graybeal holds a B.S. and an M.B.A. from the University of Maryland. As a CIA analyst, he was a member of the U.S. Delegation to the Surprise Attack Conference in 1958. In 1964, Ambassador Graybeal became a Deputy Director at the Arms Control and Disarmament Agency (ACDA), and in this position served as an advisor on the Outer Space Treaty and Eighteen Nation Disarmament Conference negotiations. In 1969–73, he served as Alternate Executive Officer for the SALT I negotiations, and in 1973–76, he worked as Special Assistant to the Director, ACDA, for SALT and as Chairman of the SALT Backstopping Committee. During this latter three-year period, Ambassador Graybeal was also the U.S. Commissioner of the U.S.–Soviet Standing Consultative Commission (SCC). In 1976–79, he was the Director of the Office of Strategic Research, CIA. Since 1979, Ambassador Graybeal has worked for the Systems Planning Corporation as Vice President, Center for Strategic Policy.

Max M. Kampelman received his education from New York University (A.B., J.D.) and the University of Minnesota (M.A., Ph.D.). His previous positions included legal counsel to the U.S. Senator Hubert H. Humphrey, Senior Advisor to the U.S. Delegation to the United Nations, and visiting distinguished Professor of Political Science at the Claremont Graduate School. Ambassador Kampelman was Chairman of the U.S. Delegation to the Conference on Security and Cooperation in Europe, held in Madrid from 1980–83. He is on the Board of Trustees, Woodrow Wilson International Center for Scholars and was its Chairman in 1979–81. He is a practicing attorney with the Washington firm of Fried, Frank, Harris, Shriver, and Kampelman. In 1984, Ambassador Kampelman was appointed by President Reagan as head of the U.S. Delegation on Space and Defensive Arms and U.S. negotiator for the current talks in Geneva.

Edward L. Rowny attended the U.S. Military Academy at West Point and holds two masters degrees from Yale University and a doctorate in international studies from The American University. He served the U.S. Army for over forty years, including a role as first Chairman of the NATO Military Committee Working Group on the Mutual and Balanced Force Reduction Negotiations. From 1973 to 1979, as an Army general, Ambassador Rowny represented the Joint Chiefs of Staff in the SALT talks in Geneva. After retiring from the Army in 1979, he served as co-chairman of the Reagan Defense Advisory Committee during the presidential campaign. In 1981, Ambassador Rowny was appointed by President Reagan as Chief U.S. Arms Control and Disarmament Negotiator and Head of the U.S. Delegation on Strategic Arms Control Negotiations. In 1985, he was appointed Special Advisor to the President and Secretary of State for Arms Control Matters.

Robert D. Schmidt received his B.A. from Mankato State College and has done graduate studies at the University of Oklahoma and George Washington University. He began working for the Control Data Corporation in 1962, where he worked in marketing and sales, became Chairman of the International Development Committee and the Export Strategy Committee and ultimately rose to the position of Vice Chairman of the Board and Chairman of the International Trade and Industry Relations Committee. Mr. Schmidt is now Chairman of the Board and Chief Executive Officer of Jacobs Wind Electric Company and President of the American Committee on East–West Accord.

Walter Slocombe graduated from the Woodrow Wilson School of Princeton University, did graduate work in Soviet politics at Oxford University as a Rhodes Scholar, and received his law degree from Harvard Law School. In 1969–70, he was a member of the Program Analysis Office of the National Security Council staff. In 1970–71, he was a Research Associate at the International Institute for Strategic Studies in London. In 1971–77, Mr. Slocombe practiced with the Washington law firm of Caplin and Drysdale, where he became a Partner in 1974. He resumed his work with the government in 1977, serving as DOD SALT Task Force Director and Principal Deputy Assistant Secretary of Defense for Internal Security Affairs. In 1979, he assumed the position of Deputy Under Secretary of Defense for Policy Planning, serving for two years before rejoining Caplin and Drysdale.

Helmut Sonnenfeldt received his A.B. and M.A. from Johns Hopkins University. He began his career as a research and intelligence specialist in the Department of State dealing with Soviet, East European, and international communist affairs. During the mid- and late-sixties, he headed the Office of Research and Analysis for the U.S.S.R. and Eastern Europe in the Department of State. From 1969 to 1974, Mr. Sonnenfeldt was assigned to the National Security Council as a senior staff member dealing with U.S.–European and East–West relations. Subsequently, he served as Counselor of the Department of State, with similar substantive responsibilities. He retired from the State Department and Foreign Service in 1977 and has since become a consultant on international affairs. He is presently a Guest Scholar at the Brookings Institution in Washington, D.C.

Howard Stoertz, Jr. received his M.A. in international relations from Yale University, after which he joined the CIA and remained with the organization for thirty-one years. Among other positions with the CIA, Mr. Stoertz served as Special Assistant to the Director of Central Intelligence (DCI) for Strategic Arms Limitation. In later years, he supplied intelligence information and analysis relevant to the SALT negotiations as Senior Intelligence Advisor, U.S. SALT Delegation. His final assignment with the CIA as National Intelligence Officer for Strategic Programs involved providing analytical support to the DCI, senior officials in the Executive Branch, and congressional committees on foreign strategic forces. Since 1980, Mr. Stoertz has worked as a consultant to the CIA and various research organizations working on national security.

Paul C. Warnke received his A.B. from Yale College and his LL.B. from Columbia Law School. After practicing law at the Washington firm of Covington and Burling from 1948–66, he became the General Counsel for the Department of Defense in 1966. Subsequently, he was Assistant Secretary of Defense for International Security Affairs from 1967–69, after which he returned to the practice of law until 1977. In 1977–78, Ambassador Warnke served as Director of the Arms Control and Disarmament Agency and Chief U.S. Negotiator for the SALT II talks. He has also served as Chairman of the Arms Control and Defense Policy Committee of the Democratic Policy Council. He is presently Partner in the Washington law firm of Clifford and Warnke, a position he has held since 1978, and Chairman of the Committee for National Security.

R. James Woolsey received his B.A. from Stanford University, his masters from Oxford University as a Rhodes Scholar, and his law degree from the Yale Law School. In 1969–70, he served as Advisor to the U.S. SALT Delegation and Program Analyst in the Office of the Secretary of Defense. Later he was a staff member of the National Security Council (1970) and General Counsel to the U.S. Senate Committee on Armed Services (1970–73). In 1973–77, he practiced law as an Associate in the Washington law firm of Shea & Gardner, before becoming Under Secretary of the Navy from 1977–79. In 1983, Mr. Woolsey was appointed a member of the President's Commission on Strategic Forces (the Scowcroft Commission) and Delegate at Large to the U.S.–Soviet Strategic Arms Talks in Geneva. He also still practices law as a Partner at Shea & Gardner.

Herbert F. York received his A.B. from the University of Rochester and his Ph.D. in physics from the University of California at Berkeley and has been a professor of physics in the UC system since 1951. He served as Director of the Lawrence Livermore Radiation Laboratory, Livermore, California, in 1952–58. Ambassador York was a science advisor to Presidents Eisenhower and Kennedy and, in 1958–61, served as Director of Defense Research and Engineering in the Office of the Secretary of Defense. In 1962–69, he was a member of ACDA's General Advisory Committee. Later, he served as U.S. Ambassador to the Comprehensive Test Ban Negotiations in 1979–81 and was also special representative of the Secretary of Defense at the Space Arms Control Talks of 1978–79. Since 1972, Ambassador York has also been the Director of the Program on Science, Technology, and Public Affairs at the University of California at San Diego. He is the author of the 1970 book *Race to Oblivion*.